T0323889

CAN YOU HEAR ME NOW?

Annie O'Sullivan has done it! *Can You Hear Me Now?* is bravely and creatively written to expose the reader to a world full of chaos and madness as she paints her canvas of her painful childhood; a world of darkness and destruction, a world of pain and the reality of growing up abused in a dysfunctional home. Annie shares her soul with us in hopes to open our eyes, and open our ears to the plight of so many abused children today. Compelling, frightening, and completely honest, Annie O'Sullivan demands our attention and we hope she will continue to do just that.

Laurie Ann Smith - Author, Child Abuse Prevention Public Speaker, No More Silence Penworks

This is a book for survivors of abuse of any type and those who love them and want to understand them. It will touch your heart and show us all we are not alone.

Eda Henschel - Reader

I must admit this is one of the few ebooks I have ever read. It was hard to read at parts, with me going through events in my life, too. I continued reading though and was happy I did. Annie gives me the inspiration to continue moving forward not only in life but in my advocacy for children. I encourage every individual to read this book.

Renee Hutchinson - President, Baby James Foundation

Raw and real, this book touches a nerve for everyone whether they've walked this road or not. Totally capturing the essence of childhood innocence destroyed and a lifetime of discovery and healing, it's a must read for anyone, whether a survivor of abuse, or an outsider looking into this hidden world that so many are living. Great reading that will make you weep with the sadness and rejoice at the inner power the author has to move on and take back the power. This is a must read.

Jeannie Short - Reader, New Zealand

What a wonderful book this is for survivors of abuse of any type. This is a book that truly touches the heart and serves to show us we are not alone. God bless you Annie for sharing your story with us. In you the rest of us can find strength. God bless...

Joan Davenport - Survivor

With life's depredations, perpetrated against the vulnerable, the Great Mystery is raising an amazing group of whom I coin "Warrior Survivors". As the chief of the Turtle Island Warrior Society, and advocate for Sky, Earth and All In Between, I also stand with these Survivor Warriors in what in all reality is a battle against the crimes of abuse perpetrated by those whom we are supposed to trust. In my journeys, I met such a warrior through Nell Cole and Fire Talk Productions/Stage Left. Her name is Annie O'Sullivan; an extraordinary human being, with Sacred Fire which burns in her.

Annie tells her story eloquently, bringing readers, or listeners, to a place and time beyond one's own realities. She takes us successfully out of the comfort zone, and into a world of such cruel reality as to make it virtually experiential. Yet, through the truth of her ordeals, this Warrior Survivor shines with strength, power and hope - not just for herself - but for all who have been through literal hell on Earth. It is a great honor to know Annie, and I know that through her story, you will come to know - and honor her - too.

Chief David Little Eagle - The Turtle Island Warrior Society

As an avid reader and supporter of survivors, I applaud Annie's willingness to look into those dark corners of her truth. Her genuine honesty awakens our common battle to reclaim our lives.

Nell Cole - Producer of Fire Talk Production

Saying I'm an avid reader would be an understatement. Rarely, if ever, has a book touched me like "Can You Hear Me Now" by Annie O'Sullivan. I found myself crying with her, angry, yelling and screaming right along with her. "Can You Hear Me Now?" totally captivated me as it will anyone who dares to read it. This book written from intense pain, abuse, tragedy and triumph; it has it all. This is a must-read you will never forget.

Becky Striblin Kemble - Rome, Georgia, Survivor

Annie O'Sullivan has looked evil in the face and lived to tell about it. Through her art, photos, and talented writing, she vividly shares her life of unrelenting sexual, physical, and emotional abuse. Other survivors will find hope in her ability to succeed against the odds. Every reader will gain an insight into this epidemic that plagues our society; therefore, having an awareness that may save a child from abuse... perhaps their own.

Brinda Carey - Advocate for Child Sexual Abuse Survivors and Author of Don't Cry, Daddy's Here

I was completely captivated by this tale. At times it is quite horrific, even more so as it is written from the perspective of an innocent, young child. The language used and the tone and detail all express this story perfectly in a way that though shocking at times, you will not be able to put it down. The strength of the author to not only have lived through and survived such ordeals but to be able to so eloquently relive these events and share them with the world is inspirational.

Suzi Davis - Author

Annie O'Sullivan has such a brilliantly unreserved writing style. It's so rare for a truly important story to be told in such a visceral and impactful way, though it must be incredibly hard to tell. I don't think I've ever seen such a bright, piercing light cast on this subject before. Thank you for that. The most important and lasting works, the ones that help countless people and contribute to real societal change, tend to take a slow but deep foothold. I believe that this story is one of those.

Lin Racher - Professional Writer

The events of her journey—incomprehensible, the evil to which she was habitually subjected—unimaginable. Yet while soberly and heavy-heartedly working my way through her painful recounting, I could not help but come away with a profound sense of astonishment and admiration: In spite of the horrors consistently heaped upon her pure young soul, the strength to survive—even thrive—is irrepressible in this resilient and courageous woman. Read this disturbing yet engaging saga; sensitize yourself to the grim reality around and amongst many of us. You will find yourself affected and changed—forever.

Mary Beth Egeling - Author of Messages from My Hands and Love-abouts. Proud sponsor of the National Center for Missing & Exploited Children

Seldom am I speechless, as I was when I finished this book. I know many survivors personally and have heard hundreds, if not thousands of their horror stories of Childhood Abuse and Childhood Sexual abuse. I have listened to them for over three decades of my own recovery from drug addiction and from the horror of my own Childhood Sexual Abuse. The stories are not pretty. The ones who tell theirs are the ones fortunate enough to survive. Many do not. Most go unreported. The remainder are seldom heard. Others suffer a lifetime of torturous silence. That Annie survived is an act of Divine Intervention in its highest form. That she talks about it is truly a miracle. That she has triumphed and thrived is almost other worldly. Her riveting and poignant story has deeply touched my soul. I am awed, honored and humbled by her presence in my life, and for her courage to share the raw and hard to hear truth of her personal experience in order that others may heal.

Bo Budinsky - Survivor, Advocate, Speaker, Author

CAN YOU HEAR ME NOW?

Annie O'Sullivan

central
avenue
publishing
2012

To my children,
who showed me how to be the child I never was,
and the mother I wanted to be.

I love you all so very much.

Thank you.

FOREWORD

February, 1992

One evening in January of 1989, I picked up a message from a distraught couple seeking therapy for the wife. A number of therapists had refused to take her military insurance coverage and the implored me not to turn them away. That was the beginning of what was for me one of the most instructive and rewarding relationships I have ever had the privilege to experience in my work as a psychotherapist.

When I met with my new client a few days later, she told me a story of such complex, bizarre, and shocking detail that I wondered how she maintained enough mental stability to arrive in my office to tell it. The telling itself was an impressive act of courage; Annie took the risk that I would not believe her. Many people might doubt for instance that a double amputee in a wheelchair could terrorize an entire family to the point of complete obedience to his every mad and cruel whim. Experienced therapists, however, have learned that stories like Annie's are usually true. We have numerous, well-documented accounts of unimaginable abuse, terror, and chaos from patients and clients whose families were dominated by one or two pathological, sadistic parents. Annie was one of many clients who have taught me about these families and the incredible resilience and inner strength of some of the children who survive them.

Over the three years of our work together, I also came to appreciate the enduring aspects of Annie's struggle to survive familial abuse. Her attempts to find stability in relationships with men had led her into a number of marriages that started well and ended badly, including the one she was in at the beginning of therapy. Her relationship with family members seemed to be ten percent promise and ninety percent hurt, as one or another approached her offering support, but eventually betrayed and denied what she knew to be true about their past. She occasionally trusted the wrong friend, overworked herself and exploded in rages she didn't understand as she tried mightily to be "normal."

In the midst of her efforts to be a good mother and to get on with her education, her growth, and her healing, Annie coped as well as she could with emotional intrusions from the past. During times of stress, she would bathe obsessively, scalding herself, going through a ritual

i

of multiple rinses, trying to wipe off the last drop of contamination from the abuse. She walked in her sleep, woke up from unremembered dreams in a state of panic, had nightmares of bloody battles and consciously wondered when her father would come and kill her for telling. She kept a loaded gun in the house in preparation for that event. Sometimes she felt suicidal. Like all abuse survivors, she worried at times that it had been her fault or that she had imagined the entire story. She also feared that anyone who came to intimately know her would eventually abandon her.

There were also the physical remnants: vaginal, rectal and urethral scarring, several miscarriages in the space of a few years, vomiting after conversations with family members on telephone, frequent gastro-intestinal symptoms, a sense of being detached from the physical sensations of her body, unpleasant memories at times during sexual intimacy and flashbacks of the pain of rape.

The major task of our therapy was to safely let Annie have as many memories of her childhood as were necessary to allow her to understand her experience as real and explainable and then to find ways for her to put the abuse and her identity as a victim behind her. She had already began this work, and as the trust between us grew, she was able to continue to tell her story and to document it with photographs, hospital records, her own writing and information provided by family members. Although to describe this work is easy, to accomplish it is most difficult. To do so, Annie had to face her sense of shame about what happened to her, the family that allowed it, the acts she'd been forced to commit and who she had been as a child. In coming to accept the child, she also learned to appreciate the ingenious strategies for survival she had developed in her early years.

We made extensive use of artwork, sand tray therapy and group therapy to achieve our goals. Her artistic talent was a major vehicle for recording and expressing her history and her inner experience in therapy.

Three of her productions come to mind when I think of the stages of her healing. The first was a drawing in marking pens done in her second group session, eight months after our therapy began. It depicts a small girl of about four or five, whose body is scarred, bloody, impaled, and disabled, who is holding bricks in her outstretch hands (one of her father's favorite forms of punishment) and who wears a pert little bow in her hair, with the caption, "Daddy's Little Girl", accompanied by a big black heart. The ironic caption summed up for Annie the denial and the deception practiced while her father committed his crimes. The picture also tells all her secrets, openly and graphically, about what was done to her. In this way, it represents the end of her own denial.

The second piece is a clay-modeled figure about four inches tall of her father in his wheelchair. In one hand, he holds his bullwhip, the other a carving fork he'd used to stab her. His blood spattered t-shirt reads "I (heart) my kids" on the front, and the back of the wheelchair bears the slogan, "Child Molester". He wears a pipe-cleaner gag. This gruesome little figure was the representation of her refusal to be intimidated by her father ever again. She immensely enjoyed that the group joined her in laughing at him, and that he was small enough to put into a shoebox and rattle him around if she wanted to.

The third piece that comes to mind is a mask Annie made when a guest artist came to teach the group how to cast body parts in plaster molds then reproduces the form in paper mache. This art form allows for great freedom in incorporating a variety of materials and colors into the finished product. Annie's mask, the product of an involved process which involved part chance, part intent, both conscious and unconscious, was both ethereal and beautiful. She expressed surprise at the finished piece, but could recognize in it her emerging sense of herself as a beautiful, strong, and gifted woman. At this point, her recovery took on tremendous momentum.

The year that followed was far from easy. Her pregnancy, as her others, was painful and difficult. Not only did she suffer considerable physical symptoms, her spouse withdrew his support. The eventual failure of the marriage challenged her newfound confidence. Her children were in distress, her nightmares escalated, some friends were loyal and some were not and our work consisted mainly of support and planning around these crises. Thanks to her efforts up to that point, she did not lose ground in her progress toward a new identity. Even at the darkest moments, her old demons appeared in her artwork as diminished, peripheral figures, no longer dominating and threatening her existence and self-respect.

Today, our sessions take place every few months rather than every few days, but Annie's struggles are not over entirely. There are memories she may never want or need to explore, and others that may demand her attention in the future. She will likely remain on antidepressants for the foreseeable future. She has a great deal of work ahead of her in raising her youngest child, and in negotiating cooperation with his father. Learning to trust and distrust appropriately is a lifelong process for Annie as it is for other abuse survivors. Fortunately, Annie is extraordinarily well equipped to succeed in these matters. Her courage, honesty, integrity, humor and creativity have carried her through the worst of times, and have enriched her life and that of those around her. She has the ability to reach out to others in need, to inspire love and loyalty in her friendships, and to speak her mind assertively.

She also had the wisdom and toughness to know that, despite the pain of remembrance, hers is a story worth telling. In writing this book, she has promoted her own healing, and potentially that of many others who will read this and recognize their own experience. In this way, she has transformed her anguish into a ticket out of the dark, high fortress of shame and isolation for herself and many others.

- Carol Lambert, Therapist

CAN YOU HEAR ME NOW?

I was told recently:
"This book is pretty in your face about the issue of child sexual abuse.
I am pretty sure people only want to hear the sanitized version of these stories."

My reply was:
"This is the sanitized version. That's all anyone ever gets when a survivor tells their story."

Part One – Confusion

Can You Hear Me Now?

It Was That Bad

"WHAT DO YOU MEAN IT wasn't that bad? What do you mean it wasn't that bad?"

I am completely outraged speaking to my brother, John. "It was exactly that bad. You tell me you don't remember that particular beating. I didn't know you were taking inventory of the beatings! My recollection is we beat feet when somebody was getting their ass beat. We left the room, got out, and made ourselves invisible. We certainly never stuck up for each other!"

When one of us got a beating all I could ever think was, "Thank God it's not me," and got the hell out of there. The guilt from this was the topic of many therapy sessions.

My brother isn't saying much and I think to myself, "Wasn't that bad? The hell it wasn't! You must have forgotten about when you and Dad tied Gabe up to the broomstick and beat him until you broke his jaw. You must have forgotten the time he stabbed me in the arm with a paring knife over a dirty dish in the sink. Oh, yeah! You didn't see it, so the scar on my arm isn't really there! You must have forgotten the time they ground out a lit cigarette out on my forehead. Oh yeah, the fork mark in my left thigh? That's not there either. Maybe the scars on my back are from things that didn't really happen because you didn't see it!"

The conversation has stopped, but my mind is reeling in my anger at his denial. Maybe he forgot the time I was out in the yard with that sledgehammer. Dad was hitting me with a stick and screaming at me to kill a puppy. I finally got scared enough and been beaten enough to hit the puppy with the hammer.

I didn't know what else to do!

Dad got angrier at every passing moment. I botched it. I was screaming, the dog was screaming and my brother came running out from somewhere and finished it. My brother beat that dog to death with the sledgehammer I had been holding.

"It was exactly that bad!" I repeated it again.

I hate repeating myself. I do it when I'm upset and believe I'm not being heard.

This is the one brother I still talk to and it is not going well.

Once again, I am afraid for my future. In my early thirties I fell apart, but I emerged from my breakdown and went on to ten years of therapy that helped me pull myself back together. Never, not once in my life, had my family been there for me when I needed someone. Now in my early fifties, I need someone, so I tried again and called John.

MY MOTHER, KATE, was a beautiful woman; raven-haired with the red highlights of her Irish ancestry. At 5'7", she was tall, slim and long legged, and built like a Barbie doll. However, she lacked the confidence one would think beautiful women have. Shy, quiet, naïve, gullible and passive, she was the perfect woman for a man like my father. Mom stayed with him for twenty-five years and left him only when her mother discovered he was cheating. He cheated on my mother my whole life. I thought husbands just did that. Grandma had proclaimed, "We are not having that! What are you doing with him?" I can only imagine my mother's reply.

Bryan was my father. He was 5'7", the same height as my mother. While tall for a woman, 5'7" was short for a man. Mom never wore heels. "It bothers your father," she would say. Otherwise, he was attractive, well built, and charming. People always liked my father. We moved around so much I doubt anyone ever got to really know him.

Dad was a violent child. He had "problems". They called him "Poor Bryan". He couldn't seem to get along with anyone for very long and was passed around the family from aunt to uncle to cousins. At sixteen, he violently raped his cousin and as was the practice back then, the courts gave him an ultimatum: join the military, or go to prison. My father joined the military, got married, and went on to breed his own victims.

The first child protection laws were enacted in 1966 when I was eleven years old. Until that time, to rape, beat, or otherwise abuse your own children, although immoral, was not a crime. People looked the other way. It was believed, and some still believe, that what goes on in your family is a private matter.

By my father's own words, I was six months old when we first "played house". I was told that I started it.

In my preteen years, during his time in the Marines, my father was in an explosion that blew his legs off and killed his colleague. Instead of being a wake-up call, the accident made him worse and encouraged his belief that nothing could touch him, since he was now a war hero.

I have three living brothers. I am the oldest. Curtis was nine or ten months younger than I and died a questionable crib death at six months. John is nineteen months younger. Gabe is seven years younger and Bryan the youngest, was born sixteen years after me.

JOHN AND I usually talk three or four times a year. I wanted to call him ever since I left the orthopedic surgeon's office thinking he would be the one I could talk to and feel better since he might understand what my body was going through. I could feel myself heading to a dark place. I thought he would be the one to understand. I was wrong.

John is a pothead of legendary proportions. He has suggested on several occasions I would be happier and less uptight if I would partake occasionally. He is married, has a child, and while he appears to be happy enough in his marriage and is making it work, he has no desire to have another child and his wife forbids him to discipline their child. John has a wildly bad temper and in his younger days, he was known for walking through glass doors. It was frightening to witness and I have been led to believe he has stopped. It is likely difficult to walk through a door if you're completed stoned.

As far as I know, Gabe is either drinking or on drugs. Decades into adulthood, John and Bryan found him and he looked terrible. He would not let them into his house, which had completely gone to hell. They saw him through the window. He looked unkempt and wild, was drinking beer and watching a small TV from a folding yard chair.

No other furniture was in the room. The front yard was a desolate tract of tumbleweeds, rocks, and dirt from lack of care. The strange thing is that Gabe's house was always one of the nicest on the street. My oldest daughter stayed with him for six months while she was attending college. He was always scrupulous about his home and the yard and took great pride in them both.

John told me he hears things through extended step family. Gabe pays support for his child, so we'll always know if he is still alive. We know that his ex-wife has had several restraining orders taken out against him in trying to deal with his temper.

I look on the internet from time to time to see if I can track where he is living. I discovered he moves a lot. He refuses to speak to any of us. He has old friends who occasionally turn up wondering if we know how to get hold of him. We don't know why he won't talk to us. Gabe won't talk to anybody, not even our mother.

His ex-wife says she can't talk to us or let us see our nephew because apparently Gabe "would go through the roof and he is difficult enough to get along with already". I lived one half mile from her house for three years and never saw her or my nephew. Gabe's problems started years ago, not being able to sleep, drinking more than he should, smoking pot; he complained of getting violently angry and blacking out. He unsuccessfully tried anti-depressants for a time before turning back to alcohol. I'm sure everything fell apart for him after that.

Bryan, my youngest brother, was a toddler when I left home, so I never had a relationship with him. I joined the Marines and moved across the country. I attempted to keep in touch. I sent letters, cards, money on holidays and his birthday. Years later I discovered, as my father was dying, that Bryan never received anything but a few cards. He chuckled about "the damn old man" taking the money.

There wasn't much opportunity to get to know my baby brother once I left home. There have never been family get-togethers, weekend BBQs, Thanksgiving or Christmas dinner celebrations. We did not return to the nest. We didn't miss each other. After my father died, I thought maybe Bryan and I could start our relationship. For a short time we made some effort, but it didn't last. Neither of us had enough family glue to pull it off, nor did we know how to bridge the gap. The lies from my father's mouth would take a lifetime to sort out and ultimately heal.

In 2004, I moved from Alaska to Nevada, and John and Bryan came out to visit. Gabe already lived in Nevada. I'd called Gabe when I first arrived in town and he was angry. I called again when John and Bryan arrived but again, it just angered him and he told me not to ever call again.

Bryan and I sort of buried the hatchet and agreed to disagree about Dad. He refused to believe that his life could have been so different from the one John, Gabe and I lived. I thought and hoped fervently that with my father's death we could heal and be a family. Oddly, even John and I now talk to each other less and less.

I HAD BEEN in a car accident. Everyone was quite sure it was just a little whiplash and that I'd be fine in a couple of days with a chiropractor and some muscle relaxers. I made an appointment with my own doctor and to my surprise, was promptly referred to an orthopedic surgeon. I was told to go see him the next day.

When I arrived at the office the next afternoon, the receptionist said cheerily, "It's the C-4 woman!" I didn't understand what she meant and waited my turn. I was engrossed in a magazine when the nurse finally called me to see the doctor.

The doctor pointed out damaged areas of my neck that showed up on the x-ray and MRI, discussing my condition. It was bad. I was under the impression the damage was from the recent accident and in seeing this, I wondered how I had walked away. I didn't have to be a doctor to see that the bones in my neck were messed up.

The doctor went on to tell me that while the accident definitely caused some of my current problems, the deterioration he was looking at in the x-rays took years to acquire. He started asking me questions – what kind of accidents I been in when I was young, was I in a car accident previously, or was it motorcycles? Had I fallen out of a tree as a kid? I told him I had been in a car accident when I was sixteen when my dad hit a tree, but the doctor discounted that when I gave him the details.

When I asked about it, the doctor said no, this was not degenerative disc disease. Having no signs of arthritis, I had to have been injured as a child to show this kind of wear and damage.

I pondered: could it have been from that beating? That day so long ago? It was life changing then; it was apparently life changing forty years later. I was obligated to think about memories I had put on the back shelf of my brain.

On that particular afternoon all those years ago, my father was in a rage. I don't remember why and accepted a long time ago that 'why' was not important. Dad's routine was to have his anger traverse into a blind, spitting rage: escalate from screaming to beatings, and later would complete his cycle with a sexual assault of some sort. When all that was done, he would practically purr his love and devotion to my well-being. It varied little. The day that I would remember forty years later in a doctor's office, was not much different.

I relived that day right there and then...

I FEEL LIKE a rag doll as he throws me around the room. The living room has a wall of glass panels with a sliding door looking out on the back yard and blood is on three of them. It matches the curtains. I saw the blood spray. It's probably my nose. I'm not surprised or alarmed. It had happened before. The difference is this time was how angry it is making him. He is screaming, spitting in his rage, "You need to clean that up!"

My father grips my arm above the elbow, kicks me with his artificial leg as he sits in his wheelchair, and punches me with the other fist. The blows to my face, back, kidneys and stomach feel as if it they are happening all at once. His arms are like a gorilla's from using a wheelchair and crutches for years. I twist and turn, only hurting myself worse. He is very strong. At fourteen, and always small for my age, I weigh in at about seventy pounds and am 4'8" and no match even for a guy in a wheelchair.

I can feel my father taking hold of my ponytail and trying to yank it out of my skull. Thankfully, the hair tie comes loose. My hair is flying all over as he grabs a new fistful and at the same time, slaps my face. More blood flies. I see it splatter the window and floor. My arm is being twisted out of the socket and I sweat both with the effort to fend him off and with white-hot searing pain in my shoulders.

My face hits the floor; I'm startled. I didn't expect it. Did I fall? Did he throw me? Maybe he dropped me and I should run for it. I don't know. I can't run. He'll catch me later and it will be worse. I can't hide, he'll just find me. He is going to kill me.

Demerol would have been nice today. No one knew my father has been giving me marijuana and other drugs. At fourteen, I am using only when I think he is coming for me. I try to outguess him, out-smart him, or outthink him. Drugs are helpful, but I didn't take them today.

I'm so tired of defending myself, having pain, and lying to everyone about every aspect of my life.

The room is too small for me to get out. The air is too heavy and oppressive and presses me to the floor like a lead blanket.

Don't move, I tell myself. A couple more kicks in the head and I'll be gone. I'm tired and feeling a little numb, which is a good feeling. I only wish I could be still and just drift off. I can't sleep if he keeps kicking me. I'm going to die here on the floor in front of that ugly bloodstained window. If I'm dead, at least I won't have to clean it up. That's okay, I decide, just let it be over. I'm not fighting. I'm not cry-ing. I am tired. I am not going to fight it anymore. I didn't know I could be so tired. He is going to beat me until I am dead this time, and I am not going to drag it out anymore; there is no point in trying to run. I can't run; if he doesn't kill me now, he'll just kill me later.

In that moment, I gave up on myself, God, family; everything and anything I'd hoped, prayed or thought might save me.

My lying on the floor like a lump infuriated him. I'm just waiting to die. I just lay there and let him kick me while he screams, "Get up!"

He can't reach me to pull me up, so he kicks me and rams into me with the wheels of his chair. I don't care any more. I enjoy being numb and I perversely and secretly enjoy his frustration at not being able to run me over. If I weren't so tired, I would laugh.

My mother is screaming as she runs out the bedroom. It's just off the living room and she is in a rage. I'm shocked out of my haze, thinking she is going to help me. I think thickly through my foggy head, "It's too late, it's too late; why did you wait so long?" I'm feeling good because my mother is going to help me. Maybe I don't really want to die after all. If she will help me, things will be different. You can think so many things in a couple of seconds.

She is screaming. What did she say?

"Get up! You get up!"

I find that I can't get up. I feel like lead. Mom is between Dad and me. As she reaches down to help me up she grabs my arm, crack! I hear it before I feel the slap on my face. I see stars as my head reels backwards from the force of the blow. This time I know I am falling to the floor. Did Dad hit me again? He's behind Mom. I'm confused. How the hell did he hit me from there?

"Get up! YOU GET UP!"

I hear this in my ear along with the buzzing. Oh God, I was so wrong. She is in a rage and she continues to scream at me, "Get up! You get up!" She calls me a little bitch. Well, I won't get up just so that she can throw me back on the floor!

I lay there at the wheels of my father's chair. I have now given up all hope. I marvel at their hatred of me and wonder why. I marvel at how long it takes to die. Dad has resumed kicking me and calling me names, and now my mother is in a frothy, spitting, screaming frenzy. I can't understand what she is saying. She is kicking me in the head! She's not helping me, not saving me. She's kicking me in the head and the stomach repeatedly, all the while screaming, "Get up! GET UP!" Well, I'm not going to get up! I lay there as if I was dead already. I give up. I won't help them kill me.

My head feels heavy and big as she stomps on it. She's trying to jump up and down on my head. Is this possible? I guess it is. Suddenly I see a brilliant, blinding, blue flash. I don't feel real pain, I think I must be past that and I am grateful. I just see the bright blue arch of light. My mother just jumped on my neck with both feet. I scream, "Just fucking kill me and get it over with!" My voice seems to come from somewhere else.

Suddenly Dad is yelling, "Kate! Kate! Stop it." It was odd, him telling her to stop. Maybe he just didn't want her to kill me; maybe he wanted to have the pleasure of it himself? Why didn't they do it together? Where are those goddamn pills he gets all the time? It would be so easy. Gray is coming. I smile. Gray is good and I feel myself disappear.

I thought I was going to die and welcomed it. I didn't want to live anymore.

I suffered that beating without medical care afterwards. Kids like me don't go to the doctor. I suffered some headaches, bruises, some sort of shoulder injury and I believe a sprained wrist. My neck and shoulders hurt, but I knew better than to complain.

I didn't think about that day for decades.

FAST FORWARD TO my early fifties. According to several doctors that I've now seen, I have the worst neck deterioration seen in someone my age. The disc is shot, mostly bone spurs remain and the spinal column is being squeezed off. They don't know what to do with me. They've all told me my condition is due to early life trauma. If left untreated, I have a neck that would one day break when I bend over to tie my shoes.

So now I'm talking to John.

My brother asks questions and then cuts me off before I can answer him. He says to go see a chiropractor. I tell him I did. I tell him they take x-rays, and then won't touch me. He says, "Well, I'm sure the doctors you're seeing are all quacks. How can they tell your neck is like that from being beaten when you were a kid? They take out little blue crystal ball?"

This is infuriating me; I'm sure he has been smoking weed but I don't ask.

After some length of our so-called conversation, my brother tells me, "Well, I have to have that same surgery in ten or fifteen years myself. It's not going to be that big a deal."

I'm furious and as I hang up the phone, say, "Are you sure about that? What did you do, take out your little blue crystal ball?"

So much for him being there for me.

I STARTED WRITING this book because I wanted people to know how it feels to be physically, emotionally and sexually violated as a child. Most people know the nuts and bolts of abuse. Most people know what it means when someone says that a little girl or boy was molested. Most people know the details without hearing it and without seeing it.

What people don't know is what went on in that child's head.

They say child abuse hurts you for the rest your life. I want you to know it's more than a memory that causes poor decisions; it colors your life, and the physical abuse causes wear you don't think about. The physical abuse goes on after you leave. It keeps going when everyone else thinks it has stopped. Something is set into motion when a person takes their fist to a child. It is a beating that can last a lifetime.

My neck is not the first medical issue I've had over what happened to me as a child. Some of it was painful, embarrassing and very expensive. There have been moments when I thought they might as well have kept me locked up in that house, gone on with the beatings, belittling me, calling me names, and raping me till I was mindless or dead.

After this conversation with my brother, I found myself angry and hurt all over again. Violated again, cheated again.

I'm a walking advertisement for what abuse does to a person for the rest of their lives. I've had physical problems too numerous to name, nightmares that plagued me for years, expensive therapy, struggles with my own children and far too many failed relationships.

And now, just when I thought I was past most of those, another one comes up.

So, yes, my brother. It was exactly that bad.

Always With Me

THE GIRL ON THE BACK of this book is me. In a manner of speaking, she is more than I am. She is my Annie Girl. She represents all that I endured at the hand of my father. I have referred to this beat-up, pathetic and pain-ridden creature as "her" or "she" for years. She was my very best friend. She was very real, very touchable and always to my right. For decades, she held on to every thought I couldn't think, every memory I couldn't bear to look at, and feelings I didn't know what to do with or want to have. She held in her small body what was inexplicable. She held all my confusion. She remembered how it felt to be me when I'd had enough. She remembered the stabbings and the sodomy. She let the horror; confusion and pain just disappear from my day-to-day reality and existence. She remembered the dead cats, shot dogs, the items forced into my body. She remembered hurricanes, closets, beatings, screaming, loneliness, and isolation.

There were bruises that I forever explained away and sometimes couldn't even tell where I got them. She knew. She remembered my father's friends when I didn't and couldn't. When the bullwhip came out, she took it, not me. She took all the mind-bending chaos for me when I could no longer bear it. She was always with me and was in all ways, always, my best friend. I don't remember my early life as a series of chronological events. They are instead a jumble of memories that come to the surface.

She, with no name is my childhood.
She, in her pain, was no longer content to remain silent and hold on to all these secrets.
She didn't want to hold all that pain by herself any longer.
I started to remember what she had kept hidden for so long.
And then, when I wrote them down:
My world exploded…

First Memories

WHEN MY FATHER GOT OUT of the Marines after Korea, he moved his young family to rural Washington and opened a diner on the road to town. We lived in an old house. I remember the window in my bedroom, a dark wooden floor and the bed, which had an off-white bedspread. It was rumpled where I had been jumping on it.

I remember a kitchen that had a staircase to my room and I remember what my mother looked like standing at the sink in a dark-colored dress and with her hair in a ponytail. To me, that is the whole house. I've learned that's how memories are – sometimes only bits and pieces, little shreds of photographs of time in our heads, supplemented by stories from people who were there at the time.

I think I was four. I was in my room but not in my bed where I was supposed to be napping, looking out the window at some cows in the pastures and singing my heart out to them. The cows were meandering across the field, grazing on lush, green grass. I climbed onto the windowsill and was pleased I could see them better. As they moved, so did I. I inched slowly across the windowsill leaning, pushing against the screen so I could see them as they slowly roamed out of my sight. I had worked my way all the way over to the other side of the sill. The screen started to give a little but now I could see them again. That made me happy. I had to move yet again to see them and the screen gave just a little. I smile and sing some more songs.

BAM!

Suddenly I was on the ground outside and screaming. I didn't know how I got there and I couldn't see the cows at all! I only saw my back yard and the two large garden snakes slithering out from beneath me. AAH, a snake! A snake touched my leg! I kept up the ear-piercing screams about the snakes.

My mother thought I was upstairs taking a nap and didn't know where to look for me while I screamed. The only way I could have gotten outside was down the stairs and right past her. I could hear her calling out my name but I didn't answer. I kept up the ear-splitting screaming about snakes – their colors, their feel, their yellow, ugly eyes! My eyes must have been squeezed shut while I screamed, because I was surprised to be abruptly yanked up from sitting. It startled me into silence for a moment and then I started screaming again.

There was a box of rusty nails on my left, a box of broken glass on my right. I landed between the two on a very large pile of grass clippings and leaves from recent yard work. My landing was so padded that I didn't have a single scratch or bruise. Mom spanked me for screaming over the snakes. I'm told they nailed the window shut later that day. I guess when I was four they didn't wish I was dead. Ten years later, they would tell me they wished just that.

That house had a shed in the backyard; it was so old, the wood was faded to gray. It had a dirt floor and windows missing their glass panes. It was wondrous inside and full of all sorts of interesting things: old soda bottles, jars full of rusted nails, screws, and other metal things. There were shiny and dull pieces of glass. There were old boxes falling apart from years of repeatedly getting wet and drying out. There were old rusted tools, buckets and things I couldn't identify everywhere. It was warm to sit in the sunny windows. I loved the mystery of all that stuff and of simply being in there.

The shed was strictly off limits. It was the first place I would go when no one was looking. I didn't do it to sneak or be bad. I just couldn't resist; it was a fascinating place.

If I jumped up and down in the dust, it made magic dust beams in the sun shining through the windows. I loved this place. I loved looking for pieces of glass to put in my treasure box. My mother had given me an old cigar box, telling me it was for treasures. I thought old glass shards were wonderful and beautiful treasures. My mother always acted as if they were precious treasure, too. I would show her my new discoveries and she would ooh and ahh over them. I always had good luck looking for them in the forbidden shed. Mom didn't know where I found them.

One day, while hunting for treasure, I came across a glass, five-gallon, empty water bottle in the shed and I knew it would make a terrific rocker.

I sat on it and rocked, side to side. I sat rocking, enjoying the sunlight and feeling good in the warmth coming through the window. I admired a piece of glass sparkling in the corner and I know I will be adding it to my collection in a few minutes. I am having a marvellous time. I'm alone and no one is bothering me. I'm singing a little song. My dog is happy too, sitting there smiling at me (I'm four. Dogs smile at you when you're four). Life is good!

POP!

Suddenly, I am sitting in the dirt – on the ground, just like that. I'm not sure what happened, but I can't move and there is blood on my dress. I'd never seen anything like that before. It was upsetting to mess up my dress. I didn't know what to do. I couldn't get up. There wasn't any real pain. I didn't understand that this was bad and I just sat there.

I don't know how, when or what exactly happened when my mother found me but she did. I was sitting on the dirt floor, impaled by a five-gallon glass bottle. She had to get me off the broken glass bottle and it must have been gruesome.

My mother was upset and yelling at me. I have a vague memory of her trying to stop the bleeding and putting me into a snowsuit to help soak up the blood. I did not want to wear it because it was summer. We had no car, no phone, no neighbors, and no way to get a doctor or any other medical facility. We lived in the middle of nowhere. My brother was too little to walk and I was very likely bleeding to death. My father was working at the diner. So, she gathered us up, and tied me into that snowsuit that doubled as a bandage, and we walked to my father's burger joint.

To get there was a walk down one very long, dirt, road. There was no traffic of any kind. All you saw for miles were hay fields along the way. I don't know if we walked the whole way or got a ride. I remember walking. In an odd kind of memory; I can see us walking down the road, my mother carrying the toddler and me beside her, half walking, half being dragged as she tried to hurry. I see it as if I am behind us, as if I am someone else watching. I watch her tell me I have to walk because she can't carry me. I watch the little girl crying.

To be fair, my mother was probably beside herself. She couldn't carry us both, and I was cut very badly, bleeding and had trouble walking.

Somehow we arrived at the diner. I was lying on the counter, and my father laughing. They got the snowsuit off and my bare behind was out; the place was full of men eating lunch. My world got very gray as they started hooting.

"Hey, O'Sullivan we get a lunch show! We'll be back every day!"

They were laughing. I was confused – I was hurt and they were laughing at me?

Everything went from gray to black. I don't know if I went home or stayed at the hospital. I must have been treated somehow, given the jagged scar and the proof of stitches across my hind end.

It was a bad day. I survived it as I would so many others.

The Trailer and The Devil

THERE WERE MANY MOVES IN my early life. We no longer lived in the old house and now that I was five years old, I slept with my brother in a travel trailer that looked like a little round pill. I don't recall my parents sleeping there with us. My parents were building a house on a hill at the top of the driveway on twenty rolling acres.

We had a white goat, Pierre, who ate lit cigarettes, blew the smoke out of his nose and thought he belonged in the house. I would beg my parents for lit cigarettes to feed Pierre. There were no doors and no windows installed on the house yet, so I didn't blame the goat for thinking he could come and go as he pleased. Once my mother blocked the door with a piece of plywood and Pierre simply turned and jumped through the window.

We still have the smiling dog.

In that trailer, the Devil used to come and get us. He would look through the window and shriek at us; he was moaning, groaning, grunting and shrieking, crying to get in while he dragged his nails slowly down the window screen. We could hear his bone-chilling laugh. The Devil's face would appear hanging upside down in the front window where my bed was. His awful face hideously lit up, hair askew and bloody, he would shriek again, MUA-A-A-AAH! Then, as if by magic, he was at the back window scratching on the screen. He was at the door howling and banging on it to let him in. He was hungry and little children were his favorite meal! We could hear him pattering on the roof and on the walls outside. He seemed to be everywhere all at once. We could see the face in the little window on the door, in the front, and at the back.

I wet the bed on those nights. I was awake. I was terrified. I was spanked for being afraid. I was not supposed to be silly. I was supposed to set an example for my little brother who was shrieking right along with me.

My father with his flashlight and his sick game thought it was all very amusing and laughed about it for years.

My grandmother used to say to me, "Always ask God for help." I thought the Devil was more real than God. The Devil was up close and personal, waiting for my three year-old brother and I to be his dinner when we fell asleep.

God was impossible to find.

My Smiling Dog

THERE WERE NO HOUSES AROUND the twenty acres that surrounded our new house. While it wasn't complete, we moved into it since it was livable. There were miles and miles of tall golden grasses all around us, moving like an ocean of gold, rolling with the breezes.

At the end of our very long driveway was a dirt road and semi-trucks sped by all day leaving behind huge billows of dust. You couldn't see across the road until the dust settled. My mother fussed about those trucks even years later, long after we moved from there. She said she always worried that one of us would get run over.

The smiling dog – I can't even tell you what that dog's name was, though there are pictures of him. I owe that dog my life, and my mother told the story for years.

I was running down the driveway toward that dirt road and she was calling after me. She could see the semi-truck coming down the road and I was on a collision course. I didn't answer her call and kept going until I was in the middle of the road. As she tells it, I was picking something up, quite engrossed in studying whatever I'd found. I stood up, looked across the street at my mother, who was yelling at me. Her words were meaningless to me, since I couldn't hear her. I remember the dog suddenly pounding into my chest, knocking me into the ditch. He scared me and knocked the wind out of me. My mother was hysterical. She thought the truck had hit me. She had seen the dog go tearing across the road and launch himself into me, but that was all. The truck screamed by without notice of any of us. My mother was racing down the driveway. When she got to me, I was lying in the ditch on the other side of the road, unharmed, bewildered, and wondering what happened. My smiling dog lay lifeless in road.

Times like that made me wonder what was I saved for.

Timmy

IHAD A NEW FRIEND named Timmy; he quickly became my best friend. I met him when my parents started building the house. He showed me how to play hide and seek in those golden grasses. Most importantly, he told me when my father was coming and showed me how to hide in the grass.

Timmy and I had so much fun. The grass was tall and no one could see me especially if I stood very still. If I crawled along the ground, I didn't have to be still and Mom and Dad still couldn't see me. They would call me and I wouldn't answer, lying in the grass under the sun, invisible in my golden sea. It was quite a magical feeling. Timmy showed me this game and I loved it.

I remember Timmy as if he were here right now. He was a little older than I was, and about two heads taller. I still remember the smell of soap and his starched shirts. He was always clean, neat, with his hair combed and no bald spots. He always wore a red and white flannel shirt. It would be tucked neatly into his jeans with a brown belt. I even remember the flecks of green in his blue eyes and deep dimples in his cheeks. He had very shiny golden hair, sun bleached white on the ends and the sun always seemed to light it up, make it glow. Timmy was always on my side, he always listened, and he tried to keep me safe.

We were inseparable and my mother often set a place at the dinner table for him while we lived in that house.

Down the hill from my house was a little creek. The trailer we slept in was parked next to it. There were trees and bushes around it. It was quite picturesque by any standard. In the summer, my brother John and I often played in it, chasing tadpoles and wading through the gentle currents.

I remember a particular day, a day when my father was very angry with me. As it often happened to me, I remember the spanking, but not the reason for it. I am supposed to be telling him something while he is beating on me. If I knew what to say, I would. I am confused; I am mute, small, and stupid. His fist hits me on the side of my head and then my stomach. Suddenly he is dragging me through the mud to the creek. I'm getting mud on my socks, and all over my dress. I can taste it. The water is cold and knee deep. The shock of it causes me to suck in air as he shoves my face into the water violently: in and out, up and down like shirt in a washing machine. My father is holding me under the water but now I am really fighting back. He has pulled out chunks of my hair. I felt the hair come ripping out; I wondered if some of my skin came out this time, since I have felt that before. Hair pulling is familiar and somehow this memory comforts me, since I know what to expect. The water is different. I don't know what is going on, what to do, or say. This is new and I can't grasp it.

I feel a snap on my face, then my arm. I think, he's hitting me with a wet towel! I've never been hit wet before. My dress is torn. I don't even know what he is saying to me anymore, much less what I should be saying. Nothing makes any sense; I am cold, and I hurt everywhere. Worst of all, I can't breathe. I'm choking on the water. It has gone up my nose and is burning. While I don't understand why exactly this is happening; on an instinctual level, as young as I am, I know I am going to die. I'm going to die right here in this freezing cold water. This is the same place where I'd just been catching tadpoles with my little brother.

I once read that when you realize you are mortal, when you understand you can and will one day die, you are no longer a child. I was five, and that was the day my childhood ended.

I believe I am dying in that creek. It is a rather matter-of-fact thought.

I wasn't sure what happened when you died, but was quite sure that this pain and confusion, this shaking and shattering feeling, would stop. You go somewhere else, right? Grandma says God comes with angels and they take you to Heaven. Life is good in Heaven. Everyone there loves you. My panic is starting to ebb. I've decided I'm going somewhere – any place is better than here. The fight is going out of me and things are going gray, white, and gray again, as colors fade in and out. I think I am disappearing because of it. The color is changing because I am disappearing. Disappearing would be good. Yes, I want to disappear and I am almost gone...

"You cunt!" my father suddenly screams.

He has let me go. I can breathe.

Timmy! I see Timmy standing there on the edge of the creek, his shoes touching the water. He looks mad, too! I don't want him to be mad at me as well! Dad's arm is bleeding a little and he is even more angry. I thought he was mad before. Now he is sputtering! I can't really hear him, it sounds like machine stuttering coming out of his mouth. I can't focus on what he is saying and he is so far away.

Timmy bit him! Timmy bit him and he let me go! I am bug-eyed with the shock of it. The pure joy and wonder of it – Timmy bit my daddy and he let me go!

Daddy grabs me by the arm and drags me out of the water, spanking me the whole way; my feet didn't touch the ground. I don't even care. I'm out of the water and I can breathe.

He is yelling at my mother and telling her, "Annie bit me!"

Now my mother is yelling at me, too. "I didn't bite him," I tell her, "Timmy did it."

She doesn't believe me and now she spanks me for lying. "Timmy would not bite your father," she says between blows.

I'm so confused I say nothing else. I've already learned that there are times to just say nothing. When I don't know what to say, it's better to just be quiet. I don't know why he is telling her I bit him. Maybe he doesn't want to have to talk to Timmy's parents. They are nice people. Timmy is never spanked. They just love him. I don't have to understand anything; I only have to get them to quit hitting me. I already know this means Daddy will come for me later and I will have to do things to him. He will take off his clothes . . . it's part of the punishment.

Timmy saved me. Timmy bit my Daddy and made him let me go. He is now my best friend for life. Timmy is brave and I will love him forever. I didn't see Timmy for the rest of the day. I had to go to bed early and without dinner, alone, in the little trailer.

Nothing was ever said about my black eye, torn dress, cut legs, scratched face, or what happened at the creek. Nothing was ever said about the chunks of hair that were missing. Mom never asked me, and though I would like to think she questioned my father, I am sure she didn't.

In my house, growing up, no one ever questioned anything. My mother never questioned anything. Dad never beat my mother's body; he beat up her mind. Too many questions would get you beat up. Don't ask. Don't tell. I think my family invented that saying.

That evening, I was pondering how brave Timmy was this afternoon. I wonder to myself if his mother got mad at him when he came home wet and with mud on his shoes. I'm wondering if he will get in trouble for biting my Daddy. He told me his parents never, ever hit him or yell at him. He was very brave to help me. I am more than a little afraid for Timmy. I am afraid he won't be able to come see me anymore.

I am sitting in the middle of the bed in my nightgown. It's white with little blue rosebuds all over and a ruffle at the bottom with blue piping. It's very soft and it's my favorite.

I am admiring the flowers and looking out the window when suddenly the door opens and there is Daddy. I didn't see him coming down the hill to the trailer and he startled me. This pleases him. He chuckles about it and is saying something about the things I make him do, shaking his head. I'm not really listening. He is always telling me that I make him do things to me. He tells me it's my own fault. I never understand and I still don't know what he is talking about. I don't make him do anything. Why does he say that all the time?

I know what he does to me is a secret. I know he will kill me if I tell what he does. I know my mother will not let me live there anymore if I tell her what Daddy does at the trailer. I know my mother hates me because I was born and ruined her life.

Daddy tells me all these things for my "own damn good". I know he doesn't care if I die. He has told me many times that no one will look for me. I'm just a little kid and no one cares about little kids. I already know that the better I am, the more I cooperate and follow his instructions, the better he likes it, the quicker he will go away.

I am five years old.

He drops his pants and calls me over. As he touches me, he is talking but I never know what he means. It's all gibberish to me. I don't care; I just want him to go away. It is in my face, touching my cheek. I hope I don't choke, I choked once and couldn't breathe, and it was scary. I start to cry.

"You brought this on yourself," he snarls. "Don't you dare fucking bite me!"

He says that I like it or I wouldn't be so bad. He says to tell him I like it. He just keeps talking to me and now I'm gone. I've become part of the screen on the little door in front of me. I'm one of the little squares in the screen, dull, gray, and square with rust in the top corner. It's over. He's gone.

The next morning is business as usual.

My eye was very swollen and ugly. I know this because my brother cried when he saw me. He was eighteen months younger than I was and he's quite afraid of me this morning. It makes me feel big and I think, "Good, you brat!" I whisper to him, "I'll get you later." I plan to feed him some mud pies with bugs later. I'm feeling a little tough this morning. I have decided this morning that I hate my brother.

I'm learning already that if you are bigger, meaner, and scarier, there is power. I was enjoying having some power over my three year-old brother. I was enjoying his fear of me. This was lost on everyone around me.

Pancakes for breakfast with powdered sugar and milk, then I went looking for Timmy out in the fields. He didn't come for breakfast that morning and I was worried about what happened to him. I found him out in the field by the side of the house and he smiled big when he saw me. He assured me everything was okay. He assured me he did not get in trouble. His mother was happy to hear what he did to protect me; she was proud of him. He tells me not to worry and wants me to know he will always look out for me, always love me, always be my best friend, and will never leave me.

I believe him.

The Playhouse

MY MOTHER BUILT ME A very neat little playhouse out of scrap wood. It was behind the house in the backyard. There was a window with a curtain, a play kitchen with a sink, a stove, and a little table with a chair. I loved to play there. I kept my treasure box on the table and pretended to cook for my dolls and for Timmy. It was a good place to be most of the time. Timmy liked it too. It was our house and our favorite place to meet.

Sometimes my father would come in all hunched over. He was too tall for the house, even with his 5 foot 7 inch height and seemed to fill it up when he entered. He looked like a giant coming through the door to my little house.

My father sat at the little table and said, "I would like to play house with you. I will be the daddy and you can be the mommy." He went on, "This is such a nice little house and we are so lucky that your mommy built it for us."

I don't want to play house anymore.

"Don't you want to play house with Daddy?" He sounds astonished and hurt that I might not want to play the game with him. I would just stand there. I wouldn't answer and this would infuriate him or he would take that silence for 'yes' and pretend to eat dinner. He would comment on how clean I kept my little house, what a good cook I was and tell me dinner was so yummy. He would ask what was for dessert, eat whatever I served up and then it was time for bed… I was the mommy and he was the daddy. It was time for bed and it was our honeymoon.

"I like this, Daddy. This is fun, Daddy, I love you, Daddy." I would be expected to say.

Daddy says, "Little girls are supposed to want to be married to their daddy. Don't you want to be married to me? What's wrong with you?" I don't know what is wrong with me. He is shaking his head in great, dramatic disgust. He is calling me bad names and then he is gone.

I'm glad he left. I'm glad I made him feel bad. I know I am not supposed to make people feel bad. I am bad. They're right: I am bad and selfish. I don't know why I can't help it and just love people.

My beautiful playhouse was ruined. I didn't want to play there anymore. Later I cried and Timmy comforted me. I was sorry I was bad. I was sorry I didn't know what to do. I was confused about why I was bad.

I do try hard to be good.

Nothing was ever said about Timmy biting my father or that I couldn't play with him anymore. Mom still set a place at the table for him. My father continued to run his diner and the story is that he had the best burgers for miles around. He had all the trucker business and I guess life was good for Dad for a while. As usual, he was his own worst enemy; he was poaching deer and mixing the venison with the beef he was buying. The health department shut him down permanently.

I was about six when I stood out in the fields talking to Timmy. It was sunny and summertime. The tall grass was always golden when I remember it. That day was no different when I told him we were moving away. I was sad and crying. Timmy was crying and he offered to let me come live with his family.

"You don't have to leave here," he said. "Stay here. My family will take care of you, don't go. Stay with me." He hugged me fiercely. I told Timmy I had to go. My father would kill me if I tried to stay.

These types of conversations went on for days, maybe weeks. It was such a long time ago, but somehow I knew I had to go and that I didn't really have any options. I wouldn't even ask my parents. I asked Timmy if he could visit me and he said no, he couldn't leave. My best friend couldn't even write me a letter and he couldn't visit.

What would my life have been like had I tried to stay? What if I stayed? That was a question I would ask many times in therapy years later.

Timmy was the best friend and playmate I would ever have. He saved me from my father down at the creek. He was my lookout at the playhouse. He taught me ways to hide and told me things to say. He gave me hugs when I needed one, he listened to me when no one else could hear me, and he loved me when no one else did. I still miss him on occasion.

Timmy was my best friend, my guardian angel and my saviour. Timmy, who I can still remember so vividly, was my imaginary friend.

So Close to Normal - Yet So Far

I HADN'T BEEN IN SCHOOL before. We moved to California and I was going to be in first grade. I joined the Brownies and I loved it. I loved my teacher. I played with kids at recess. I sold Girl Scout cookies and got to spend the night at a friend's house. My teacher told me I was smart!

We lived in a duplex within a few blocks of the ocean and my mother would often walk us down to the beach. I loved walking on the hot sand and feeling the waves roll over my toes. I hunted for shells and my brother I buried each other in the sand. We built sand castles with moats that the surf would creep up to fill in. Life was good here. My uncle and cousins would come to visit. We made friends with twin boys that lived next door. Dad's family lived in southern California and an uncle was a manager at a local hotel. He would save us the Disneyland tickets that guests left in the rooms. It was a kid's dream: free tickets to Disneyland! I loved California and wished Timmy could see it.

Daddy still visited my room, but I didn't care anymore. It was just part of life. I think it happened to everyone and I just had to live with it. I wasn't any different from anyone else, except that I was a bad person.

My father's temper got worse. One day when I was in second grade, neither John nor I can recall what set him off. He beat us with the belt, which set off tears and wailing. This chaos set him off further, causing him to force us to strip naked, then, get on our hands and knees and crawl to a spot in front of him. He swung the black belt in his hand.

"You are pigs. Say it!"

"We are pigs."

"Wrong! Who's a pig?"

"We are!"

"I'm a…" I don't hear the rest of what he says as my face hits the coffee table. The pain above my eye is excruciating. I lift my hand to touch it out of reflex. WHACK!

"Did I tell you to touch your face?" Another blistering strike across my back with his belt. He has the buckle out swinging now.

"No, Sir!" I cry out.

"I will tell you when to move, what to touch, and how to touch it! If I say jump you will ask how high! If I say shit you will ask what color! I am your God and you will do what I say, you will think about only what I want and what makes me happy. You exist only because of me. You owe me for that! Who is a P-I-G, pig?"

He swings hard and it's a blistering strike to John's back. He got it first and I can see the welt swelling, red and burning already. I started to get up to run as I see my turn coming. It's a rare for me to think to run away and I hesitate. Before I can even get to my feet, my back is on fire. I can't get away now. The pain is burning and while still comprehending the first hit, a second rains down on me.

"Don't you dare fucking run," he says. "I always know what you are thinking! Do you think you have an original thought in your head?" We have heard this speech before. "You don't have a thought in your head that is your own. I know what you are thinking before you ever think it!" We have managed to gain control and now we are both silent on our knees listening. My brother no longer exists. I can't even see him or hear him anymore. He is erased from my head, my life, and my existence. It's now survival. Survival did not include taking care of my brother, nor him taking care of me. We took care of ourselves.

"What are you?" he bellows.

"We are pigs!" We cry out in unison, trying to give him what he wants. The belt whooshes down again, this time in slow motion. I know I'm a bad person. I know I'm going to burn in hell. I don't care about my brother, my mother, or about God who has abandoned me for all my badness. I only want to get away and somehow make it stop. I need the pain to stop. I am shaking and I can't stop that either. I'm out of control, I must stop shaking. Do not cry! He hates it when you cry. He will beat you more if you cry. He will beat you until you stop crying. Do not cry! Okay, I'm not breathing but I'm also not crying. If I take a breath, I will cry some more. He is talking again, not really yelling; it's a menacing, snarling and dangerous sound that is coming from him.

"Not 'we' you dumb shits! Say, I. Am. A. Pig!" He tells us in a condescending voice. "And make a piggy noise!" He cackles.

In unison, as if rehearsed, we stutter out, "I-I-I-I a-am a p-p-p-ig. Oink, oink."

"Oink, oink, what?" Another strike of the belt. I am melting from the pain now and my mind completely blank. I don't know what to say. I just look at him afraid to say anything that could be the wrong word. I said what he told me. I'm confused. My mind and my face are blank with stupidity.

He screams. "Sir! SIR! SIR! I'm a pig, oink, oink, SIR!"

I hear the belt whistle but it doesn't hit me this time and I am grateful. There's no empathy, I'm only thankful it wasn't me.

He laughs again, and I see my mother, but she is silent. She came out of the kitchen and she's standing there. She doesn't stop it. She is watching. I have no time to think about her. He is laughing again, "Crawl around the coffee table, say, I'm a pig, oink, oink. And keep going till I get tired!" I am crawling. "Quit that goddamn whining and crying or I will really give you something to cry about."

My knees hurt from the braids in the rug and they begin to bleed. We have come around past him several times and he hits us with the belt each time we pass. Now he is angry that we are not crying.

"Think you're tough, eh?" He is sitting on the sofa and he pushes me into the coffee table with his foot as I go by.

Oh no! What is the answer? I don't know! Am I tough? Does he want yes? No? It's a trick question and I can feel the panic setting in. He was calming down and I thought maybe it would be over soon, but he is getting louder and I can hear the frenzy in his voice. My head is screaming at me, he is screaming at me and I don't know the answer! What's the answer?

I am starting to move to a new level of panic. He has moved to the other side of the sofa. It is near a vase that has peacock feathers in the corner. The feathers are gone from the vase and he has them in his hand. I'm confused. I think he is going to hit me with the peacock feathers.

"Bend your dumb ass over the sofa."

I blink. "Huh?"

"Get over here and bend over on the fucking sofa – are you deaf *and* stupid, you little cunt?"

I get up and begin walking over to the sofa, and he shoves me to the floor.

"Crawl over!" He is screaming. "Who do you think you are, walking in front of ME?!"

I don't answer so he hits me again with that belt.

I am crawling; my world no longer exists for me. I am alone. Moreover, it's black, with just me and my father's hands.

We are both bent, our faces in the sofa cushions and still naked. Suddenly, there is pain like fire. Blistering pain! I think I am on fire. I think he is shoving a lit cigarette up my bum. I didn't know you could do that.

"My butt, my butt, my butt!" I cry.

Suddenly it dawns on me what has happened. He inserted those feathers in our rectums, and secured them with tape to ensure they stayed.

"Crawl." He snarls. "You'll cry now, you little fuckers." And we did. We sobbed! Then, as was more familiar to us, he beat us until we stopped. The grand finale of this event was that I was told to go outside and walk down the driveway so that everyone would see I was bad. Everyone would now know what a little cunt, whore, and troublemaker I am. No one would be friends with me any more because I was a pig.

He opened the front door and shoved me out. I am looking around. I'm naked, beat up and have feathers stuck in my backside. I am so worried that someone will see me. It doesn't occur to me that I might get help if I am seen. I only think everyone will know that I am so very bad. My shame is complete.

Finally, my mother says very softly, "Bryan, that's enough." He relents and tells me to go to my room and get dressed. He tells me he will deal with me later. My brother has disappeared already. I don't even know if he was outside with me. John told me later he couldn't remember anything past the coffee table.

That night, Daddy comes to my room locking the door behind him as he always does. He looks at my bruises and welts. I'm scabbed over now and sore when he touches me. I have many welts and bruises and though I don't know it yet, I will not be going to school the next day.

"I don't know why you make me do this to you," he says. I just look at him. I have nothing intelligent to say so I decide to just keep quiet.

"Daddy loves you more than anything and it hurts me to hit you like that." He continues, "You know that, right?"

I nod yes.

"You know you're my little girl and I love you more than life, right?"

"Yes," I say.

"Yes, what?"

"Yes, Sir."

"Take off that gown and come over here."

He is sitting on my bed with his pants down around his ankles.

"Take it." He touches me.

I do what I have to do and fade into my gray mist. The next day, it's all forgotten.

I don't know what to say about my cuts and bruises when I do go to school, so I just say I fell down. I think everyone believes me. I think everyone believes I deserve whatever I got handed to me.

I'm no longer allowed to go to Brownie meetings. The leader tried to talk to my parents but it did no good. Dad said I was bad and didn't deserve to be in Brownies and I didn't deserve to be with those normal, nice kids.

Moving to Massachusetts

MY THIRD GRADE TEACHER WAS the best. She wore suits with heels. She swept her hair up into a fancy twisted bun. I thought she was beautiful and she never knew how important she was to me. I got to sit with the smart kids. She thought I was smart and she gave me things to do that proved it to myself. If you got good grades and turned in your assignments, you got extra privileges. She made me feel so good about myself that I desperately loved her and would do anything for her. I would only have her for half the school year though, until we moved to Massachusetts. It was the beginning of the Vietnam War and my father was going. Mom wanted to be with her family on the east coast while he was gone.

We arrived at Christmas. Seems we always moved midyear, and we always moved about the same time people began to ask about my bruises. I assumed they asked my brothers the same sorts of questions. My brothers and I never spoke of it. Those topics were off limits and still are off-limits.

We dressed up in our good clothes as people did in the sixties and got on a plane to Massachusetts. I felt very special in my black patent leather shoes and my new dress, bought especially for this trip. My Uncle Clay took us to the airport. He was my father's brother and at the time a pilot for Continental Airlines. He was a beautiful man inside, and with movie star good looks. I was going to miss him so much. He called me his Princess and I believed I was.

Uncle Clay had travelled in Africa and told stories about the animals, natives, and plant life. He was an amazing storyteller and I was a child in need of a fantasy. I hung on every word he said. He and I were going to live in Africa. When we got there, I would be a princess. That was who I really was. He would be bring my crown soon and I would see it was true. We would live in a giant strawberry and eat only the most delicious of fruits and have no worries. Being the princess, everyone would love me and only want to make me happy. I would wear beautiful hand carved wooden and bone bracelets. I would have no chores and I would always wear beautiful clothes. I believed him. I needed him to tell me those things. I needed a magical place to live in my mind that was so different from my reality. He didn't know that; he just liked to tell me stories and play make-believe with me.

My mother got angry with me for talking about the crown. She would inform me that my uncle was telling me stories and he shouldn't, since I wasn't going to get a crown. "You are not a princess!" She would tell me sharply. "You are not going to ever go to Africa and live in a strawberry! Stop talking about it!"

He was just being my uncle and I think he truly cherished that. I know I cherish the memory of those stories.

The Vietnam War Brings Happiness

MY FATHER WENT OFF TO Vietnam and my mother, John, Gabe and I were in Massachusetts. My maternal cousins, grandmother, aunts, and uncles were all there. My mother's sister lived in the house they grew up in; my grandmother on one floor and my aunt and her family on another.

We had Christmas together before my father had to leave. Overall, it was a good time. Dad only got me alone in the basement once the whole time we were there. I suppose there were too many people around. I became great buddies with one cousin in particular and we quickly became inseparable.

I didn't realize it at the time, but I was about to embark on the best year of my childhood.

We ate fish on Friday, chicken on Sunday, and spaghetti on Wednesday. I went to church around the corner from my house and was in the church variety show. Two other girls my age and I dressed like cats and sang, "We Are Siamese If You Please" from the Disney movie *Lady and the Tramp*.

We jumped out of windows at that church playing Mary Poppins with our umbrellas. Our mothers put a quick halt to that.

There were trips to New Hampshire, Revere Beach, Mauldin, and the homes of relatives.

We spent the summer, or at least the better part of it, at my great aunt and uncle's house in New Hampshire.

Upon arrival, in the low light of early evening, bats flew out of the attic. The house had been closed up for months and our arrival caused them to come flying out. My brothers, four cousins and I ran around

38

screaming hysterically. We thought the bats would get in our hair and make us crazy. My mother and my aunt ran around behind us telling us to shut up, quit screaming, the bats would not eat us, make us crazy, or stick to our hair. It must have been a sight to behold.

The woods surrounding the house were all birch trees with beautiful white bark. We would get up early in the morning and run around in the woods.

We found out there was a swimming hole if you followed the path in the woods. The swimming hole was our favorite place, with some of the coldest water I can ever remember. My uncle told my brother and me that he went down to the swimming hole every morning and threw ice cubes in. John and I got up every morning and raced to beat my uncle to the swimming hole so that he couldn't do it. It was great fun. My uncle laughed every day with us about it.

We made friends with kids who lived around us. We had barbecues, we made birch canoes with my mother, we saw ski lifts, and best of all we saw the old Man of the Mountain, a natural rock formation in the mountain that looked like the face of a man. My mother made sure we saw the sights, heard the history and all the folklore of the area. I suspect this was much how my mother grew up. There are many pictures of my mother with her family on all her travels.

I discovered that year, the year I was in fourth grade and thanks to my cousin, that not everyone took their clothes off with their father. This was a revelation to me, never spoken of again, but I thought about it from time to time.

While I was happier at home, school was not going well for me. In California, they learned multiplication at the end of the year; in Massachusetts they taught it at the beginning of the year. I was so behind; I couldn't catch up. I didn't like my teacher. She told me I was stupid and should be held back a grade. I was used to getting good grades and didn't know why I was having so much trouble with my work.

I was frustrated and so was my mother. She tried to help me with my schoolwork to no avail.

Things were good at home, with normal sorts of punishment for the usual sorts of kid stuff.

My father had been gone to Vietnam for nearly a year and I hadn't thought about him. I heard he was coming home soon.

One day, my cousin came over and as I remember it, we were peeling apples for my mother. My great-grandmother is sitting at the table with us, shredding paper for the cat box. She's been very ill and is staying with us. The knives my cousin and I have are sharp, and I say to her, "Let's see who has the sharpest knife." She puts out her wrists and I press the knife to her flesh. Then I put out mine, she presses the knife into me. I feel no pain, although I can sense the sharpness of the blade. She puts her wrist back out and I touched a knife to her flesh again, no reaction. I don't want to hurt her – I love her. My mind starts to turn; next time it will cut me. It won't hurt.

Out goes my wrist, the knife leans into it, and as I feel the pressure, I pull my wrist away with a smile. I say, "You win." I look in fascination as the blood sprays. I was right, no pain. My cousin turned white and my great-grandmother blurted out something as she stared with huge, saucer-like eyes.

No one ever asked what we were doing or what I was thinking. It was just another accident in my life. Mom and Grandma tried to figure out what to do with my arm.

My thoughts during all this were of how easy it would be to stop living, stop existing. What just happened, happened in an instant. I wasn't sophisticated enough to understand it was suicide, a sin, or even slightly wrong. I only knew I wasn't happy.

When I pulled my wrist away, my mother and grandmother had been talking about my father coming home for Christmas.

As happy as I had been during our time in Massachusetts, I no longer wanted to stay there.

I Can't Remember You

ONE NIGHT AFTER DINNER THERE was a knock on the door. My mother asked me to go answer it and there in the door, in full uniform, stood a smiling man I didn't know. The screen door was locked and it was dark outside. I told him we were not interested in buying anything. I slammed the door in his face and turned off the porch light.

Before I made it down the hall there was more pounding on the door. My mother came running out of the kitchen, wanting to know what was going on. I told her that a salesman is at the door and he wouldn't go away. She opened the door to see what the problem was. She was smiling and let this man into the house; he is screaming at me for not letting him in. I was dumbfounded. This went against all the rules. Strangers, especially strange men, did not come into our house.

The man was yelling at me, so I yelled back, "Shut up!"

My mother was horrified. The man is stunned, and raised his hand to strike me.

He said something to me, and I said, "You are not my boss and I think you should get out of my house."

He grabbed me by the arm and began to shake me. My mother stopped him by saying something quietly. Mom smiles and says brightly, "This is your father!"

I stared at him and said, "I don't remember him."

My mother said, "What is wrong with you, of course you do!" John jumped for joy and toddler Gabe was also excited. I wasn't happy to see this man like everyone else was. I am crying and he, my father, spanked me.

I remember that time like this: I'm in my room crying because I don't remember my father. I think he's a bad man. I think he tricked my mother and she let him in the house. Then he took off his belt and reminded me exactly who he was. My mother tried to tell him I needed time, I was just a kid, but it didn't matter and in the end, she didn't stop him. The belt blistered my backside.

A few days later, my father acquired a car and we have gone off in it one evening. He talks to me as if I'm an old lover he's come back to visit. I don't remember my father, but I do remember vaguely the things he used to do, and make me do.

I know I don't want to do those things.

I say, "I don't remember, I don't know what you're talking about," and, "can we please go home now?"

He could have walked away that night and pretended that none of the past ever happened. He could have changed the course of my life, his life, but that isn't what happened. He wanted me to remember, and he reminded me in Technicolor. He reminded me that I said it was fun. He reminded me that I said I liked it. He told me he had missed me more than he had missed my mother. He told me how he had a little girl my age living with him while he was overseas. She liked it as well. She took good care of him, cleaned his house and washed his clothes, too. He asked me, "Don't you want to be like her?"

This is not going well for me. I believe if I just kept telling him I didn't remember, he would stop. I'm a year older and now know this is not normal. Nevertheless, there is still no way out of it for me.

We parked somewhere outside of the city lights; my father sat in the front seat of his new car with his pants off. He grabbed a handful of my hair with one hand and twisted it so tight that it hurt and I could not pull away. With his other hand he took off my clothes. As he shoved my face into his lap, I just disappeared. I didn't even have to see the gray first, this time.

The Gestapo Games

SHORTLY AFTER DAD CAME HOME from Vietnam, we moved to North Carolina. I was nine years old and this was a particularly bad time for me. The violence escalated and the games Dad played became more complicated. I started to realize I lost time. I thought it happened to everyone.

I began to be accused of and punished for things I didn't do, and even worse, accused of being "seen" doing them. I could only say, "I didn't do it" and still suffer the consequences. Sometimes, to escape a beating for lying, I would plead guilty to the crime and was beaten anyway. They were indeed beatings: a fist, belt, sticks or anything nearby to inflict pain was used. These could never be confused with mere spankings. Dad assured me it hurt him worse than it did me and it would have been worse if I had lied. He went on to lecture in a gentle, understanding voice that telling the truth was always the best thing. The only constant in my life was inconsistency; the beatings were never for the same reasons. Life never made sense and was becoming vague in ways I couldn't understand or articulate.

We moved into a house on the bay in a small North Carolina town. There was a house being built on one side of our house and on the other was an older mobile home. A boy named Charles and his mother lived in that mobile home.

A boat slough came nearly all the way to our house. It was rough looking – a great gouge in the earth full of water from the bay, no decking or dock, and only mud paths up to the shore. Tied to the roots or big rocks sticking out from the sides were the boats. It was usually full of water moccasins. There was some form of a beach; in reality a stretch of mud, weeds, with a shack down near the water. It was all very rustic and we were told nearly daily to stay out of the water or the alligators and snakes would get us. John and I swore we saw alligators on a regular basis; however, most, if not all, of the alligators were old logs floating in the water. The water moccasins, however, were very real.

Right next to the shoreline at the front of our house there was a drop-off into much deeper water. We found an old rowboat sunken there, and soon discovered we could stand on opposite ends and make it rock like a seesaw. We thought of it as our underwater teeter-totter.

It was inevitable one of us would get hurt. We got it rocking one time and I slid over what was most certainly a rusty nail or boat trim and it ripped through the skin on my ankle. I still have a nasty scar from it. Woolly Boolly carried me, as I bled all over him, to my mother.

I don't know what his real name was, but Woolly Boolly lived in a shack down by the water, and we were not supposed to talk to him. He had wild hair matted like a sheep, he liked to fish, and all the locals claimed he was crazy. John and I liked him and he didn't seem crazy to us. He lived alone.

Woolly Boolly was always nice to us. He showed us how to catch crabs. Sometimes, he would give us strings baited with chicken necks to catch crabs as well as a bucket to throw them in. We thought this was great fun.

We would sneak down and swim on a regular basis, usually right in front of his shack, always careful to yell and scream and throw rocks into the water first, as he had shown us, so that any snakes would be frightened away. "Those snakes don't like you anymore than you like them. Let them know you're coming," he told us in his thick southern drawl.

This was the sort of place people dream of for raising families. It was rural. Dirt roads and bus rides to school. It was a place where kids could grow up playing in the woods and learn to sail. You could pick berries in the summer. You could swim in the bay. When it rained in the summer, it was a warm rain. The sky would just open and it would pour down. I loved being out in that downpour, splashing in the mud then running into the water of the bay.

You could dream if you had a minute and you knew how.

Or, you could play hide and seek.

Daddy had a new favorite game. He learned it in Vietnam; it was a form of hide-and-seek, called "Gestapo." Daddy was the Gestapo; my brothers and I, and any friends we had around, had to run and hide. If the Gestapo found one of us, he could torture us with whatever form he chose. I learned a new word, torture. Before this, we didn't know what that meant.

At first, it was just my brothers and I playing. Later, Dad got Charles, the boy from the old mobile home next door, to play. Charles was about our age, a little chubby from staying indoors too much, awkward and quiet. He didn't have a dad. After a few games, he didn't want to come out to play anymore. My dad went and talked to his mother. His mother said it would be good for him to play with other kids and forced Charles to come out and play with us. It might have been fun if it had really been a game. I doubt Charles was having much fun.

I would never know what went on with the other kids who played this game. What the Gestapo, always my dad, did to his victims was a secret and part of the game. The other kids always quit playing. Sometimes mothers would send them out to play with us anyway. My father was a smooth talker and most of the time they would come back for a while. The mothers liked my dad. They thought we were lucky to have a dad like him.

Daddy assured us torture was part of the game. The Gestapo were the bad people and they had to torture the people they caught. I could not quit. If I quit he would tell my mother who already hated me. If I quit, he would remind me, "She will make you go away to live at the parochial school and then you'll find out how good you have it here." Daddy always knew how to get what he wanted from us.

Once when we were playing Gestapo, he took me to the empty house next door that was under construction. We were forbidden to enter this house. On this night, he told me he had special permission to use it. There was a light coming in through the window from the porch light at our house so I could see fairly well. Once in, he took me to a closet, stripped me of my clothes and hung me by my wrists with his woven belt. I was old enough now to feel the shame and humiliation at being naked. He was talking; I felt the gray and started to hear a roaring in my ears like the ocean.

"Love," he said.

I hang there, watching his lips move, but there is no comprehension. I catch a word here and there, but they make no sense to me. The roaring is so loud!

The ice pick came out. It wasn't the first time I'd seen it, but I couldn't remember what happened before, or why I wasn't surprised to see it. He gives me a little push so that I begin to swing back and forth. My wrists are burning and my arms and shoulders ache from hanging. My feet don't touch the floor. I see the ice pick and he came at me with it. He keeps pushing me so that I am fully swinging.

Prick!

Each time I swing towards him, I get stuck with it. Prick.

He is talking. "Gestapo." I can't tell what he is saying. The roaring is too loud. Prick. "Good." Prick. "Tell me." Prick. "Say it!" Prick. The roaring is louder. I am in a panic! Say what? I can't hear! I can't talk either. The gray is coming and I think I will disappear soon. The world around me became darker in the already dim light.

Blackness.

Nothing.

Whatever else happened, it's gone from my head. I never remembered, not even after years of therapy, not in hypnosis, never. Magically, I was back in the house listening as he told my mother I fell in some terrible thorn bushes and what a clod I was.

My parents had an argument with Charles' mother. At some point, I believe she accused my father of some things. Nothing ever came of it. Nothing ever did. As he told us so many times, he was "God." Charles didn't play with us anymore and we only saw him on the bus to school.

We still played the game with Daddy. I stopped remembering being caught. Just like the night in the car in Massachusetts, it was more lost time.

My Magical Bedroom

I LOVE MY BEDROOM IN the new house. The rest of the rooms were disjointed like rooms pieced together from several houses. I remembered the front door of the house, but never going through it. We could enter the living room from the front door; however, I can't tell you what that room looked like. I remember a bathroom with a white toilet, but no sink, shower or walls. My parents' room was somewhere down a dark hall across from my brothers' room. I couldn't remember any other room, save the kitchen; there was a sink with a sunny window over it.

This bedroom of mine had a rug in the middle of the floor. There was a picture on the wall. A couple of stuffed toys were usually on the floor and on the bed, and there was a toy box on the floor under the window. The sun spilled in through the curtains and caught the dust particles, making colorful sparkled beams from the window to the floor. If it wasn't God, it was surely fairy dust or angel dust. It was magic, my magic.

I loved my bedroom. I didn't share it with anyone. Sometimes when the sun came through the window, I sat there in the warm light on the rug and prayed. Grandma told me I could always talk to God. That room was so warm and felt so magical when the sun came in that I believed I could. God could hear me in this room.

I prayed for my dad to go away or at least break a leg and leave me alone. I heard you could ask for a sign. I asked for a sign that life would be okay. I promised to put the sign on my wall and tell other people. Evangelism, tent meetings, and revivals were everywhere in the Deep South. It worked for others, why not me? I just had to be a good girl and God would look after me.

Dad had never been in my bedroom. It's mine. I didn't have to share it and I was safe in there. Yep, yep, yep. Life was going to be good in this room, a magical room with sunbeams and moonbeams. Only me, myself and I could be in there. I thought, too bad Timmy isn't here. I miss him.

I liked the way my sheets felt and they smelled good when Mom brought them in off the line. I fell asleep hugging my bear, thinking about my good luck. I thought, Daddy couldn't come in here. Yes, life would be good in this room.

HEY!

I'm being pulled out of my bed by my hair. I can feel it coming loose from my head. I hit the floor with a thud and my head bangs on something; my head hits the corner of something and I think I feel blood coming down my cheek but there is no time to think about it. It's dark. I am trying to get up, tripping over my nightgown and I get a fist in my face, then into my side. As I try to twist away, I slip on the rug. It's my praying rug! How can this happen on the praying rug?

I make a run for it, going who knows where, just going!

My father grabbed my wrist; I know I'm not going anywhere. I'm awake now. I do not know what happened. I don't know why he is hitting me in the middle of the night.

"You didn't get me up!" Dad has my arm in his grip along with my nightgown and shakes me until my teeth chatter. My head is bouncing back and forth and side to side. I am trying to focus. I can't. I just stare. I'm blank. I can't think. I can't talk. I don't know what to say. All I can do is listen to Dad screaming at me.

"You didn't get me up!"

My alarm didn't go off yet – oh no! What happened? Panic is rising now as it begins to dawn on me that he got up before I did. My job is to get Dad up in the morning. He goes to work early in the morning. I get him up; make his English muffin with peanut butter, jelly and butter. I take it to him and then I am free to go back to bed until it is time for me to get up for school.

"You didn't get me up you stupid fu…" I don't hear the rest of the sentence as another smack across my face knocks me to the floor and my hip burns where I hit the wooden floor.

I'm crying now and holding onto my face, still not talking. There is nothing to say. I'm nine. I don't know why the alarm didn't go off; maybe it did. I'm trying very hard to remember why I am supposed to be here, what he is talking about, and what the answer is supposed to be. There is no answer. I can't concentrate as he tosses me around my safe, magical room. It's dim and gray. Maybe I'm still sleeping. Why isn't the light on?

As if to let me know I am not sleeping, he hits me again. The screaming, shrieking, and spitting goes on as he hurls vulgarities, threats and accusations. I think about the spit spraying me more than the words. He roars at me, "I will get in trouble and then I won't have a job and it's all your fault! Your family won't have a place to live because of you! I have to be at work on time!"

I just want to get away from the pain. He just keeps hitting me and screaming. My head is pounding with my heartbeat and my chest hurts. Something is bleeding, I think maybe it's my chest; later I discovered it was my nose.

The light came on! My bed is in a shambles. The blankets and sheets are on the floor. The rug is in a heap in the corner opposite the door. I see my father standing over me, sweating and breathing like a dragon with his hands balled into fist.

"Bryan! Bryan! STOP!"

I hear my mother and try to comprehend her sudden appearance in the room. I am astonished! Mom is yelling at him. He is telling her I didn't get him up and now he is late for work. He is screaming at her now and she screams back as if he is deaf. "Bryan, she is just a little girl!" Wow, she is so brave! She made him quit! He is still yelling, swearing and calling me names, but he has stopped hitting me. I'm not listening to them argue anymore. I am happy they have forgotten me for the moment because they are yelling at each other. This is still a bad situation since they could both turn on me in a minute.

He storms from my room, brushing past my mother who follows him. Suddenly he whirls back at me and in a low nasty voice and growls, "You will pay for this later. I won't forget and I will get you for this!"

I just stand there.

As Mom followed him out of the room, she told me to go wash up and go back to bed. "You have school tomorrow." I did too. Washed my face and went to bed. I couldn't get my bed put together and so slept under a pile of tangled sheets and blankets.

I am living in the moment and this moment is over.

He is furious. His parting words, though a little bone chilling to an adult, meant little to me. I wasn't sure what he meant but assumed it would be nothing new. He would take off his clothes, talk about why I was so bad to make him do it, and then it would be over.

I know I sound casual. I didn't look forward to it. It would be awful. I would cry and I might even beg, but it was inevitable. It was part of my life. I knew I couldn't tell and that was all that mattered. It was part of the punishment. Being beaten and raped was going to teach me what it is like to be a grown-up. When I cried he told me, "I don't know why you're crying, you make me do this to you."

My shame of being such a dreadful person was crippling. By now, I know in my heart, that I am a horrible, awful person. Even God was ashamed of me. The truth is I had no idea what to say if anyone asked me. If there were no words in my vocabulary for what had been going on so far, then what would happen later that day was far worse, would be incomprehensible for years and the physical damage would be permanent.

I got up, went to school, gave some lame, 'I fell down' excuse for the new bruises. The "Don't Tell Rule" was enforced regularly. If I told, my father would kill me. I believed him. He also made sure I knew no one would believe me if I did decide to tell anyone. "You're a kid," he would say; "Who do you think they are going to believe?"

This was about the time people started thinking that maybe you shouldn't be doing anything you wanted to your children. Though it meant nothing to me at the time, the first child protection laws were enacted this year, and I was attracting some attention with my bald patches and bruises. The new thought was maybe children shouldn't be coming to school with marks on their faces, arms and legs.

I had a male teacher that year and he was always asking about the bruises. I believe he was honestly concerned. He made a mistake in calling my home and asking about me. My father gave me a beating for not telling my teacher a better story. I had not told my teacher anything except that I had fallen down. It was what I said to teachers as long as I'd been in school. I fell down. I didn't have a better story. No one ever gave me one to tell in the first place and I didn't know what Dad was talking about. The teacher stopped asking me how I was acquiring bruises when I came to school the next day with new ones. I was learning that people might ask questions but they couldn't do anything but make it worse for me. That teacher was my first lesson from outside the family.

"They will never believe you. You are just a stupid kid." My father's lecture would start. "I am your God. I made you and you owe me for your very life. Those teachers you think care about you, don't really. They believe me and not you. I can kill you and no one would know or care and your mother would be glad. She is jealous of you and she finds you disgusting. She wishes you were never born to ruin her life. She wishes you were dead."

I can hear you thinking the question as you read this: Where was my mother during all this? I don't know. There were times I didn't think she was even real. I didn't question her position. She hated me; she wished I wasn't born to ruin her life. She was the enemy and certainly not someone to be trusted.

That morning, only a few hours after being dragged from my bed, I went to school and had an uneventful day. I remember we played baseball and I had to change my clothes. I came out to PE with shorts on and my teacher asked about the bruises again. I told him I fell out of bed. He asked if I was sure. I was terrified of the conversation he is trying to have. He looked at me sadly and said, "Okay, let's go play some softball; you can be first base – you're the best first base we have!"

I was nine years old and in love with my teacher from that day on. He was always very nice to me, asking how I was that day and telling me I was a smart girl. He told me I was smart in spite of all my failing grades. He knew I was smart and he knew I just had very important things to think about. He was right about that. I was thinking about staying alive, staying out of the way and how not to go home. I guess he didn't really know what to do about the situation. Mornings were great. I loved being at school but I just didn't have the concentration to get my work done. After lunch, I would start thinking about going home and my lack of attention grew worse. He was right; I had more important things on my mind than Christopher Columbus.

That day, the day of my early morning awakening, I was especially tired and distracted. I was sure my father was going to beat me some more when I got home. I was sure he would be waiting when I got there. What if he was soaking that belt? I hated it when he soaked that belt.

I got off the bus and soon discovered he had indeed come home early and was waiting for me. Mom was in the kitchen when I got there and I saw him give her some money and tell her to go shopping for something. Off she went. She left me alone!

"Where are my brothers?" I ask warily.

"They are out at the neighbor's, playing," he snarls. "I've been waiting for you."

"Oh."

I don't know what to do, but he fixes that right away.

"Get to your fucking room."

I go to my room and sit on my bed. I'm not sure what is going on, but I have the sense to be afraid. In he walks with a stool he brought from somewhere. I have never seen it before and watch as he sets it in the corner. He leaves me waiting for him to return.

I wonder what the stool is for but know better than to ask aloud. I am completely fixated on the corner.

I'm startled when he comes in, telling me brusquely to take off my clothes. The tears start. I know this isn't supposed to happen. I'm off balance and confused. There is something different about all this and I don't know what to think.

"Get on the stool and face the wall."

"Huh?" I try to buy some time. This angers him further and he slaps me hard enough to knock me down.

"I said get on the fucking stool, you stupid cunt!" He screams at me now. "Quit crying, no one can hear you." That also means no one can hear him. No one can hear me!

My mind is reeling. I am getting on the stool to be hit some more. Why on the stool? This is my magic room! God is in this room! What if I fall off the stool?

He keeps knocking me to the floor. I know I'm going to be knocked off the stool to the floor. He chased God out. I want to say something, anything, but I can't speak. All I can do is obey him and hope for the best. He has worked himself into a frenzy and I'm too slow and clumsy for him. He keeps hitting me to speed me up, but it makes me more awkward. He is making fun of me for falling down when he knocks me to the floor. I just get up and try to continue.

The stool is in the corner of the room. The door is off to my right and the door is even still open! The door is never open when he comes for me. My magic had abandoned the room because he left the door open. I finally fumble my way onto the stool and stand on it facing the wall.

He growls, "Put your hands on the wall and bend over!" I do it thinking about the belt, the wet belt. I'm shaking thinking about it but I have no comprehension for what is to happen next. I look for the belt but don't see it anywhere.

Grease! What! WHY!

I'm terrified and I say nothing. I see him putting it on himself. I can't say it or even think the word. Grease? It's Vaseline for the babies. What? Why? I don't get it! He wants me to see him do it. He turned the stool some so I couldn't help but see what he is doing. I don't comprehend and his crucial moment is lost on me and angers him.

"Do you know what I'm doing?"

I shake my head slowly, not taking my eyes off him.

Now he is smiling, "Turn around, hold the wall and bend over."

Suddenly there is white-hot searing pain. I'm screaming! I'm crying for help! I'm dying! He has hold of me and won't let go. I can't see anymore. My body is being slammed into the corner of the wall over and over, hitting the top of my head, then my face as I squeal and twist to get away. The pain is unbearable. I'm nothing but a forty-five pound rag to him as I try to fight my way out of his grip, the relentless pounding and this blinding pain.

Suddenly it's over. There is still pain and there is blood everywhere, there is blood all over my legs. I still don't know why. I still don't know what happened to me. He dumps me on the floor; apparently, he no longer thinks he needs to hang onto me. I can't walk very well. I'm now on the floor, on my knees, and quite speechless.

Rags materialize and he throws them at me saying, "Clean up this fucking mess. I can't believe you made this mess. For Chrissake! Clean it up!"

I have forgotten that I am even naked and start cleaning up the floor and the stool. He walks out of the room saying, "I'll be back and this mess you made had better be cleaned up." He is subdued now but still clearly angry.

He comes back a few minutes later and sends me into the bathroom to clean up. I can't. I am finally sitting on the toilet as I have discovered that is where the blood is coming from. I'm mystified why I am bleeding like that. I'm not sure what to do about it. He makes me bend over again and I start to shake. He laughs and tells me to relax; he isn't doing that again today. He puts some sort of salve on me and tells me to get dressed.

I'm crying and trying to get my clothes back on and he leans in the doorway. "Quit snivelling, this is what it's like when you grow up, so you better get used to it."

I vowed to myself at that moment that I will never grow up. "You better get used to it" has echoed in my ears ever since.

My mother got home shortly after and she called me to help carry things from the car into the house. As I came into the kitchen, she stopped short and asked, "What happened to you?" She is looking at me hard. She never really looked at me, but today she did. "What's going on, what happened to you?" she repeats. She never asked before. I tried to tell her. I was going to tell her. I just stood there looking at her, mute. I had no words. I don't know what just happened to me. I don't know where to begin. I was helpless.

Daddy came strolling into the kitchen, and while I was standing there looking at my mother, he suddenly puts his hand on the back of my neck and squeezes it hard. It hurts. There are already bruises there too; I can feel the tenderness as he touches my raw skin, digging in his fingernails for good measure.

"Oh, hell," he says. "She was just being bad; I took care of it, Sugar. Don't worry about it. You know how she is, always doing stupid shit."

Mom looked hard at me again and I was still trying to form something to say. I couldn't. My brain was seizing up as I struggled to form a word or thought I could say aloud. I stood there hopelessly mute, knowing my chance is over.

He said to me, "Get out of here, we don't need you in here ruining our day and messing up our life. Go outside."

She never asked again, and by the time I did have the words, it was too late. My father had convinced me that she knew and that she didn't care.

We Don't Live in the House Anymore

I DON'T REMEMBER ANYTHING ELSE until we moved to the trailer park. My magical, beautiful room was gone. When I asked about the trailer, why we lived there now, what happened to the other house, my mother got annoyed with me for asking stupid questions. "What's the matter with you?" She asked. I quit wondering and just figured it was all part of life; things change. Sometimes you know the reasons, sometimes you don't, but don't ever mention that you don't understand.

There is something wrong with me. They tell me I'm stupid. My father tells me this is how life is for every little girl. I would not risk asking the wrong questions. Even the right question today might be the wrong question tomorrow. It's just best to keep my mouth shut and believe whatever they tell me to believe today.

I don't remember my favorite teacher, going back to school, packing or moving. Nothing. I don't recall months at a time. I simply woke up and my world was changed – teachers changed, homes changed, my hair would change. I didn't look for signs anymore. I didn't try to tell anyone anything. I stopped asking God for help and I quit praying.

All my mother really had to do was look at me, hear me, see me somehow; but she couldn't. She might have saved me – even in some small way. I didn't know how to make her, or anyone else for that matter, hear me or see me. I was trapped in my own ignorance, naiveté, and in the lies and threats that were part of my life.

If I got too bold and caused my father any fear, he escalated the threats of death, lectures of who God, my God, really was. If I became sullen, he would punish me by masturbating in my face, want me to do it for him, rub himself on me or want a blow job. By now, I knew what a blow job was, I knew what 'get bent over' meant, but I didn't know what a period was or how a girl got pregnant.

As is prone to happen in the Carolinas, and not long after we moved into the mobile home, a hurricane was coming. I helped my mother tape the windows of the trailer so they wouldn't shatter, and someone helped my mother tie the trailer down. We were busy getting hunkered down for a big storm. The wind was whipping and the sky was black. Trash was blowing around outside. It wasn't terribly cold, but I recall the dark and the endless whistling wind.

I was helping my mother inside with water jars when Dad came in from work. He said he needed to go to the store. Mom argued weakly with him that it was bad weather for a car ride anywhere and probably not safe. Of course, he won. I had listened with interest of a child listening to something that doesn't really concern her.

Suddenly I heard I was going with him! I felt my stomach fall. I didn't want to go out there into a big storm. They told us all about it at school. This is not safe. Furthermore, my Dad is not safe either.

I was trapped and it was too late. I could argue, but I would just get a beating with the belt. Maybe the buckle, maybe a fist, or worse, something would be slammed into my body. There would be more bruises to explain and hide.

I resolved to just get it done. I would just go to the store. I would help get the groceries he wants and get home. We would do it fast and then I'd be home – safe. It would be okay.

My mother was still protesting, but he didn't bother listening to her. We went out into the hurricane.

I was looking out of the car window and thinking about the car being sucked into the air like the in The Wizard of Oz when I hear Dad say, "You know, we aren't going to the store."

"Huh? Where we going?"

He laughs and says, "I've missed you."

I've heard those words before, my heart skips a beat, and my chest hurts. I know better than to say anything. I finally noticed he wasn't driving toward the little store, but turned onto a tractor road in the cornfield.

Why didn't I think of this? Would it have mattered? No! Even if it had occurred to me that this would be my fate in the middle of a hurricane, it would have changed nothing. I would still be sitting in this dumb car with my heart pounding, with no place to go. I couldn't run. No one could hear me, though by now I didn't believe anyone could or would help.

The storm is closing in; rain is pelting down on the car, lightning is flashing and the thunder is crashing. The wind that was picking up when we left is beginning to howl eerily through the fields. The dirt road is quickly turning to a river of mud. I'm not sure where I am. If I did run, he would kill me when he caught up with me, or he will tell my mother what I did and she would kill me. He's told me repeatedly that only he loves me, and my mother hates me. That I need him. I'm trapped like a rat. No, not a rat, a rat could scurry away and hide. I'm worse than a rat. I'm afraid. I'm disgusting. I'm ten years old.

He parks the car and grabs my arm to pull me over to sit by him. His pants are open and I don't even know how the y got that way.

"Tell me you like this," as he grabs my hair and shoves my face into his lap. I have to say things to him. He tells me what to say. If I don't say it fast enough he will slap me and pull my hair some more. I guess I resisted and he slapped me again.

"If you bite me, I will kill you. I can. No one would ever know. I will leave your little fucking body right here in the corn field as fertilizer and no one will know. What makes you think you are worth looking for? You're not, no one will care."

I'm crying and that satisfies him that I believe what he's saying. I do. I believe even God is afraid of my father.

He hands me a washcloth that has appeared from nowhere. Now he is nice to me, hugging me and says in a jolly voice, "Let's get home, there's a storm out. But, first I got something for you."

He pulls a big white shoe box out of the back seat and sets it in my lap smiling and looking very pleased with himself. I'm confused.

"Open it!" He demands happily, expectantly. There in that box are a pair of white go-go boots I had been coveting for months. He is happy to give them to me. I put them on and I don't know what to say. I just sit there looking at him. He smiles and says to me, "You earned them; your mother won't understand, I'll take care of that though." I remain silent looking at my boots.

My mother was angry when she saw the boots.

She yelled at me over them. My parents fought over it. I heard her yelling about her being his wife and wondered why she said that. I didn't ponder it for too long. Of course, I didn't tell her how I earned them, and neither did my father. By the time I was ten, I knew better than to tell anyone anything, especially my mother. I learned from the incident in my old bedroom that she wouldn't ask too hard. If she did, I wouldn't have the words to explain anything, anyway. I didn't know how to say what was happening to me and had been convinced by Daddy that no one would believe me. I was just a kid. I was his kid and he could do whatever he wanted with me. I guess he was right.

I slept in those boots. They were mine.

Yes, indeed, I earned them.

Can You Hear Me Now?

Part Two – Understanding

Can You Hear Me Now?

Fishing Trips

ILOVED CATCHING CRABS WITH a chicken neck tied to a string. Down on the bay, at the end of the pier, we lay on our stomachs and hang out over the water. Crabs loved the chicken neck hanging in the water. The smellier they got – the better the catch. Crabs would swim over and latch on to the chicken neck with their claws, and then we very slowly and carefully hauled them up and shook them off into our waiting buckets of sea water. Occasionally one would fall off and go back into the water and we all would groan. Sometimes one fell off onto the pier and scrabbled around our bare feet before plunging into the water; something that was always sure to get us squealing and jumping around.

It was common for the little fish hanging around at the end of the pier to come and chase after the chicken neck. We thought the fish could smell, because they sure came around for that rotten old neck! Sometimes we caught them and watched them swim for a while in the buckets, then dumped them back into the water later to go free.

I sleepwalk. When I do, sometimes I head for the bay – I loved fishing that much! I escaped so many times in the middle of the night that Mom installed bells above the doors. The ringing never woke me up, but it sure got Mom running after me. Once I headed to my best friend Nancy's house to see if she wanted to go down to the pier at one o'clock in the morning. My mother caught me running up the road in my pajamas just as if it was midday.

School was almost out for the summer and I was going flounder fishing with Nancy Hamilton and her family. What a night it would be! The water was very shallow where the flounder buried themselves, so there was no fear of drowning if we fell out of the boat. Of course, we quite merrily fall out of the boat and into the warm Atlantic Ocean at every opportunity.

I was in paradise. The water was warm on my body and the ocean sand soft on my feet. Nancy's dad was laughing and telling us, "We will go hungry with all of you fishing like that!" But, we kept falling out of the boat to swim and giggle wildly. We knew there was a cooler in the middle of the boat packed with tuna sandwiches, cookies and Kool-Aid. Mr. Hamilton handed each of us a flashlight and a cookie and we settled down to do some serious fishing – hanging over the sides of the boat.

We switched on our flashlights and intensely watched for the flat fish. We leaned over the sides of the flat-bottomed boat, our flashlights hovering close to the surface of the water.

Occasionally someone would squeal, "Fish! Fish!"

We were all looking for the sandy silhouette of the funny, flat fish buried just under the sand. If were really lucky, it would be laying there 'waiting to be dinner,' as our boat captain said.

"Fish! Fish!" Nancy called out.

Her father shuffled over to our side of the boat to have a look. He studied the water for a minute, his gigging pole held high. We all held our breath expectantly and shone our flashlights on the water for him. Suddenly, he stabbed into the shallow water with his gig, triumphantly coming up with a fish. We squealed in excitement as he brought up a flounder.

He warned us in his pirate voice, "Doon't be rockin' the boot; doon't want to end up in the drink do ye?"

He praised all of us for our magnificent hunting skills, and then declared, "We will all eat tonight, me little mateys!"

His silly antics delighted me. "This is the best night of my life!" I burst out.

He laughed as I quickly returned to the side of the boat with my flashlight, earnestly hanging over the side looking for the biggest, Moby Dick-sized flounder in the sea.

EVERY OPPORTUNITY I got, I went and fished off the end of the pier hoping for another boat trip. My next opportunity to fish from a boat turned out to be with my father. This was unexpected, since he never allowed any of us go with him. I heard him say all the time to his friends that Mr. Hamilton "is a dumb ass for taking all those kids fishing!" His rant continued with, "I don't know how anyone could catch fish with all those damn kids around!"

So, I was excited – this was going to be an amazing night. I get to go with Daddy and his buddy, Chuck. Only me! None of us kids ever got to go, especially at night. I was so excited!

On our rowboat, we are going gigging for flounder just as I did with Nancy and her family. I had so much fun with the Hamiltons that I can't think about anything but the fun we all had. Chuck is going too and will be no further away than the other end of the rowboat. I am not going to be alone with my father and I get to go gigging!

Daddy's rowboat is a little wooden dinghy, weather beaten, mostly seaworthy, in need only of some sanding, minor plugging up and paint. The last trip out I got splinters in my bare leg from sitting on the bench seat. The motor rarely works; making the oars our most important tool on the boat.

One time, the motor quit and he was angry with my brother and me. He yelled at us about the motor and blamed us that it wouldn't start. He screamed that it was our fault for getting in his way. While he paddled back to shore, we both bailed water. None of this mattered to me now; it is a boat – and I am going to be on it.

Big ole Chuck will be there so there's no risk. I'm safe tonight. I'm going to get some fish and I'm so happy!

Chuck is a big, southern guy; tall and stocky. For a Marine he's a little chubby and is always on the 'fat-boy' program. Daddy doesn't think it's fair for Chuck to be called fat because he can run and he is strong like an ox. He is a really nice guy and he is my dad's best friend. My mother is friends with his wife. They have three kids the same age as my brothers and me. We all play together, and we go on outings with their family sometimes. I'm the oldest of all the kids. I will be in the fifth grade in the fall.

It's warm out and the water is warm, too. Daddy keeps yelling at me to quit hanging over the edge. I'm dragging my arms through the water and thoroughly enjoying myself. I can't drown. The water isn't deep where you gig flounder. Chuck laughs every time Dad gets after me.

He says the same thing I am thinking. In his slow southern drawl, he says to Daddy, "Not nuff warder to drown in, bubba. Quit yer yappin' at that purr youngin'."

Daddy and Chuck are talking about work or something equally uninteresting. I am lost in the feel of the wind, the salty, fishy smell of the ocean and the spraying water. I continue to brazenly defy my father and hang over the boat trailing my hand in the water. I am without a care. Chuck is here.

It is a very rare and carefree moment in my life. No wonder I remember it so well.

We land on a sand bar. It's almost an island out in the middle of the bay. All three of us are out of the boat. I am having a great time fishing in the warm water with my flashlight. I sure love the water. I'm not paying attention to what Daddy and Chuck are doing.

Hey, Chuck is leaving with the boat! I'm only ten years old, but I've been on and around the water most of my life. I know enough about tides, and I'm alarmed. My heart is starting to pound and I don't feel so good. Chuck is leaving us on a sand bar while the tide is out! It's dark like black ink. The moon is out and you can see the reflection on the water; but land, I don't see any land. It's like there is nothing out there, just this spot on the water where we are.

"Hey Daddy, why is Chuck going? Why is he leaving us here?" I'm not hiding the panic rising in me very well at all. Daddy thinks this is funny. I go on to tell him as if he doesn't know, "The tide is coming in and he left us here!"

In the blink of an eye, my night changed.

A minute ago, it was exciting to be out. A minute ago, I was having the time of my life. A minute ago, I was safe!

A minute ago, Chuck left my dad and me on this sand bar to fish.

I have my flashlight but we don't have a gigging pole.

Where did Chuck go? How does Chuck think we can fish like this? The tide is coming in!

We are in the middle of the ocean at night with only a flashlight! I thought this fishing trip was going to be fun.

I am good at avoiding being alone with him. Now, I'm alone in the ocean with Daddy and I don't know what to think.

I can't think anymore. I can't put anything together.

My thoughts are racing out of control while I try to focus on what is happening. I have no focus, as questions and ideas race through my head. All that is left is chaos and questions that I know better than to ask out loud.

How can this happen? I am so careful.

Isn't the tide coming in? I am going to die out here in the water.

Could I swim home? It's dark. I don't know where to go.

Aren't we in the middle of the ocean? No one will find me.

Is this true? Am I actually, honestly, alone on a sand bar in the middle of the ocean with my dad?

Why did Chuck leave me here with my dad? Chuck must be a murderer!

Who takes a boat away in the middle of the ocean when the tide is coming in?

The fish will eat me. Dad once told me I would make good fish bait! WHY?

I am so trapped! I feel like one of the bugs that my dad likes to rip the legs off. He laughs and laughs while they scramble around. Did I hear laughing just now?

I can't comprehend what is going on as my brain travels down various routes trying to make sense of the situation. Things are too far out of context for my limited experience.

I can't get my balance. There is nothing I can say or do. I feel the squeezing in my brain and I know things are going to get gray in a minute and I will just disappear.

Daddy is showing me how to fix my pole so that it won't get lost in the water or dragged off if I snag a fish. Where did that pole come from?

I thought we were here to gig fish, not pole fish. I didn't bring a fishing pole, did I?

There's no tuna sandwich here. I think I'm sleeping, and this isn't real. However, I know it is real. I'm awake. I struggle to focus. I'm afraid that if I can't pay attention, I will drown out here.

I can no longer tell the difference as my real world fractures and the surreal sets in. I don't wonder what is happening to me. It has happened so many times that this is familiar and I find a sort of twisted comfort in it. The tilting, the gray, the fogginess, the squeezing of my head; those are not the problem. It's uncomfortable when the squeezing starts, but never painful. It's only momentary; then the world blurs. It's much the same as falling asleep.

It's that moment before you slip away into the void of dreamland for the night. When you wake up it's over.

It's vague, like the remnant of a dream and I forget about it. I don't make a connection between being and not being. I don't dwell on my lack of memory. I never dwell on the experience I have been able to circumvent in this way. I very nearly embrace the empty space.

My clothes are coming off. Daddy's clothes are already off. How did that happen? Mystified, I wonder where his clothes are.

I'm in the ocean.

My brain snaps open and shut like a camera shutter, a moment passes and I disappear into another. Still pictures of what is going on flutter in front of me as I lose awareness of time. I don't understand. There is massive confusion.

I can't run, hide or stop anything. I feel all. I'm stuck in between. Now, I can't talk. He is annoyed with me. Did he just ask me something? Maybe he is just talking. Somehow, I know he is asking me something but I can't put enough sounds together to comprehend and I don't answer. I hear him from far away, as if his voice is coming through thick mud bubbles.

Blub, blop, blurb.

I can't understand. It's disjointed and disconnected; the words I can make out are of no use to me. I can't make sense of them. He hits me now because I can't answer. I don't have to answer anymore. I'm gone.

I lose time. I simply believe this is the way we all live. I can lose a day, a week, and a month. I will wake up somewhere else, equally confused, however, I will be having a better time when I wake up.

I'm told I caught three fish that night.

I'm told I insisted that Chuck call me 'matey' the rest of the night.

I'm told I sang pirate songs and laughed while the boat sped home.

Everyone laughs as they hear the tales of how much fun we had and how I talked of being able to go again. I'm told I was a 'really, really good girl' last night.

If anyone had asked me all those years ago, I would have said I don't know any pirate songs. No one asked me if I had fun that night. No one asked me anything.

They just tell me what I am supposed to remember . . . and then I say that I do.

The Explosion

DAD RECEIVED ORDERS TO GO to Guantanamo Bay, Cuba. He was going to be gone for six months. I only cared that he was going to be gone. I wouldn't miss him. I couldn't wait for him to be gone. I hated it when he was home. They told me all the time that this kind of thinking made me selfish and inconsiderate. I guess I was just a bad person. I couldn't help it. They all hated me. Dad said he was the only one that really loved me.

My mother didn't trust me and the feeling was mutual. Mom told me that being pretty was not going to pay the bills. Dad told me that being pretty would get me everything I wanted. He also told me that he was teaching me what it would be like to be a grown up and 'get bent over'.

I didn't ever want to grow up.

My mother hated me. I knew, because Daddy told me that all the time. Mother screamed at me all the time, "I hate you, I wish you'd never been born! You have ruined my life!"

Once she said she had to love me because I was her child, but she didn't like me. She wasn't even mad at me that day. I, alone, was the cause of my mother's miserable life.

Daddy said the day I was born, it ruined her life. He also said, "Mommy is jealous because I love you more than I love her."

Daddy also said he loves me and it hurt him to punish me the way he had to. He wished I wouldn't make him do that.

"Mommy can't understand people like you and me," he lectured. "We are future people. That's why you have to keep secrets. Regular fucking assholes that are out there in the world don't understand that

70

we are future people and we think differently."

That was the conversation I had with my father before he went to Cuba for six months. Happy as I was that he was gone, I was also left with a mother who wished I were never born.

I don't know which is sadder: that my mother hated me and I was being left with her, or that I believed Daddy was the only person on my side.

A FEW MONTHS later, as I got off the school bus at the corner, I saw the chaplain's car in front of our trailer. It was a short walk down a gravel road to our place. I didn't know what to think. Every member of a military family knew that the chaplain at your house meant bad news, really bad news. I didn't know what to expect. Other people are there too. My mother is talking to someone and is very upset. No one paid any attention to my brother and me as we walked in the door from school.

There had been an explosion. Mom was going to Jamaica. She was leaving us here! She told us Dad was in an explosion. They didn't know if he was alive or not. The lady from the Red Cross was there, too. She told us we were going to stay with Nancy's family. Nancy is my best friend and I thought that was fine.

My brother and I asked in a single voice, "What's Jamaica? Is Daddy there?"

"Jamaica is a place," Mom says, trembling. "No one knows if your father is there for sure but that is where they want me to go." Her hand was shaking as she lit another cigarette.

Nancy's mother appeared and was telling us to get some clothes. "Hustle," she said. "Everyone is going to our house now." As I turned to go to my room, I glanced out the window.

"Hey, Mom is getting into the chaplain's car and leaving! Did she even say goodbye?"

No one answers me.

I looked around and Mrs. Hamilton waved me off to get my things. "Your mama has a lot on her mind right now, it'll be okay. Go get your things and come on."

I didn't care. As I went down the hallway, I realized that he wasn't dead – I knew it. He was the meanest man alive. He made deals with

God. Even God is afraid of him, I think with contempt. I am certain of this. I see it as a fact based on my experience.

He won't be dead.

A few days passed without any word from my mother. Mrs. Hamilton was preparing supper. Nancy and I were playing with Barbie dolls in her room. My brothers were in the front room with the other boys, watching TV.

Mrs. Hamilton called me into the kitchen and asked me if I was concerned about my father.

"No." I think this is a strange question.

She had asked me that a couple of times. My answer remained unchanged and it appeared to bother her a bit. "We will talk about things after dinner," she says.

Nancy's parents skipped dinner and were in the living room with the TV turned up so that we couldn't hear them talking.

Nancy said knowingly, "They have something big to talk about."

I asked what it was, but she doesn't know. "That's how they talk about things," she said with a wicked grin. We finished dinner and rose to take our plates into the kitchen.

Mrs. Hamilton spotted us and with a quick glance at her husband, she told me to come out to the living room and to bring my brothers with me. She had to tell us something. Maybe my mom was coming home? I slung my baby brother Gabe onto my hip and washed his face quickly before he could screech at me that he liked a dirty face.

We were all sitting on the sofa in a line. Mrs. Hamilton explained to us that my father had been in an explosion in Cuba and he lost his legs. It was bad, but he would live. John was crying now, and that set off Gabe. I just look at her.

This is quite beyond anything I could comprehend. I remembered when he got his appendix out. He had a huge scar. You could live like that. I remembered how he came outside of the hospital to see us wearing a white and blue robe and sunglasses. He showed us his scar. It was ugly.

Mrs. Hamilton was telling us that one of Daddy's legs was gone at the knee and the whole leg was gone on the other side.

I was horrified and mystified. I screamed, "You're lying!" I screamed it repeatedly. "You lie! You lie! You lie!"

She was trying to touch me, she wanted to hug me and I jumped back screaming again, "Liar! Liar! Liar!" I couldn't stop saying it. This was not expected. I didn't know what I was expecting, but not that! Not a horrible, sick, ugly lie that I could not comprehend. Why was she saying that?

I was running around the room now because I didn't know what else to do. She didn't know what to do, either. I couldn't let her touch me or something would happen to me.

"No legs? NO LEGS!" I screamed.

My brain was cramping and the tilting gray was starting, but for some reason I was stuck between the two. I didn't go anywhere – I just felt disoriented, off balance and confused. "No, you lie!" I insisted. As Mrs. Hamilton came close to me, I screamed, "No, don't touch me!"

My brothers were crying now, adding to the pandemonium. She couldn't catch me as I darted around the room hysterically.

Finally, I ran out the front door. I ran around the trailer park, then down to the cornfields and back up the road again, down to the water. I didn't know how long it took me, but the sun was starting to set; I was perched on the end of the pier watching it. I had worn myself out running and I had trouble catching my breath. There was a horrible pain in my side.

If anyone came for me, I would jump in and swim away! I hated them for telling me this stupid, awful lie.

You couldn't live with no legs! Everyone knows that. Not possible. Stupid woman; why did she tell me that? I hated her. I hated her whole family. I hated my stupid crybaby brothers, too. They cry and the grown-ups liked it. Makes them feel important, as if they have something to do. I kept my power; I didn't cry.

I sat there alone, looking at the water, talking to the birds and the fish.

I was calm now. It was getting dark but I didn't want to go back there to those awful stories. Suddenly, Nancy was beside me. "My mom told me to come find you; I figured you would be here."

"Yeah, here I am."

I liked the water. I like counting the little waves and the ripples. I like watching the little fish under the pier and counting them. I like everything about being on, in or around the water. I even like the smell of the ocean which, as I'm told by many adults, is like the smell of dead fish. I feel peace here.

After a few minutes I asked, "Why did your mom say those things?"

"She says your mom called and that's what she got told. She says it's just awful."

I cried out, "You can't live with no legs, she made a mistake!"

There are a few minutes of silence as we both mull over what we are being required to accept.

Nancy finally broke the silence and startled me with her sharpness. "Well, I don't know how you can live like that either!" A few more minutes passed as we watched the sun sink into the water.

In a near whisper, she said, "My mom says you have to come inside now."

We started the walk back to her house silently. Neither of us really grasped what all this meant, nor did we know what to say.

As we turned the corner, almost there, Nancy looked back at me and said solemnly, "I promise, my mom doesn't ever lie."

I thought to myself that all grown-ups lie, but I kept it to myself. I know that Nancy loved her parents and that they were not like my mom and dad. I knew she would be angry with me if I told her what I thought. Some kids are like that. I had learned already that kids had to stick up for their parents, even when it meant saying their parents weren't hitting them. So I didn't argue. I shrugged my shoulders and quietly followed Nancy back to her house.

I walked into the house without uttering a sound to anyone. I didn't know what to say. I didn't know what to ask. I didn't know how to look. All this silence bothered Mrs. Hamilton and she asked if I have anything to say. I thought she was looking for an apology and I told her, "No." She peered at me from over her glasses as if she didn't understand my reply. I think she wanted me to say something else. I was lost.

I brightened a tad as I told her, "It's a mistake. You can't live with no legs." I'm sure she didn't think of that.

She was sitting in her chair and I could tell she was looking for the words to say to me. I stood there for a minute; my discomfort was obvious as I decided not to wait: I was tired suddenly; I was so tired that it was hard to turn and slowly walk down the hall to the back bedroom. My legs and arms felt like concrete blocks as I walked into that gray sideways world of my personal void.

All I thought was, I am going to bed early tonight. I'm so tired.

One day I wake up.

That is the only significant element I have for you, for anyone hearing me now. I wake up. Rather, it is in the vein of waking up.

I have missed an afternoon, days, weeks and maybe even months. I don't know and have no way of knowing.

I come out of a fog, slowly becoming aware of being on the school bus. It's like waking up on a lazy Saturday morning after sleeping late. I'm not sure what is going on. I'm warm, and I'm not sure if it's morning or not. Hmm, nope – it's afternoon; I can tell when I look out the window. The light is hurting my eyes and I am going home. I rub my eyes and sit up straighter on the bus seat.

I begin a sort of inventory. I don't think I have seen my father. I am on the bus coming home from school. I am vaguely aware; I am supposed to go home to my own house. My mother will be there, so she must be back from her trip to see Dad. I can hear a lot of laughing around me and I look around, not sure what is going on. Everyone is looking at me expectantly.

They are laughing at me! It suddenly dawns on me – that little jerk Robby is sitting at the back of the bus, making fun of my father, my family and me. Me!

"Hey!" he says, "Your daddy ain't got no legs. Your dad gonna walk around like a crab on the beach? Gonna flop around like a fish on the pier?" Now he is laughing hysterically with his friends. "You can't sit in your Daddy's lap anymore, cuz he ain't got one!" Everyone is dissolving in front of my eyes as they laugh at me – except for Robby.

I lunge at him like a rabid dog.

Before I even think about why, I am on him – hitting, kicking, biting, pulling his hair and screaming at him. I don't know why I am so angry, but Robby is getting the beating of his life until the bus driver drags me off him.

The driver tells me with a chuckle, "You are just a bitty peanut of a girl and you are gonna get hurt beatin' up on them boys. No good gonna come of this," he drawled.

I wasn't afraid of fights. I wasn't afraid of Robby, who is yelling at me through his split lip, "I'll get you for this, you white trash whore!"

What was some kid going to do to me? Hit me? Push me? My dad beats me with his fist and he is grown. My brothers and I hit each other with sticks and chase each other with knives, shovels and pieces of two-by-fours.

"Pfft! You think you're gonna hurt me? Ha!" I scream, and try to wrench out of the bus driver's grasp. "I'm gonna kill you and feed you to the fish for bait!" I was unquestionably going to make him think twice before he made fun of me again.

I can't get loose no matter how much kicking and screaming I do. The driver is well over two hundred pounds and has to duck to get on the bus. He has all fifty pounds of me under his arm and he is hauling me off the bus yelling at the rest of the kids not to move. They are all sitting like mice now, some wide eyed at the spectacle playing out in front of them. Robby is whimpering in the back and his friends are making faces at me.

The driver continued to carry me around the waist in one arm until we were away from the bus, and only a few feet from my house. He set me down on the dirt road and waved at my mother, who was in the front yard. She saw us and realized something isn't right. She started walking towards us. In that instant, in pure determination, I tore off running for the bus again.

I was like a spitting wild cat when the driver got hold of me for the second time, lucky for Robby.

"I am gonna beat his ass! I am not finished beatin' him!" I screamed.

The bus driver is afraid to let go of me and other parents have gathered near the bus, curious about what is going on and why their own kids have not gotten off the bus.

The bus driver was talking to my mother while I was still in a foaming frenzy. Mom was embarrassed by my obscenities and screaming. The driver wouldn't let go of my arm, nor did he put me down as he told my mother with a chuckle, "Not to worry, it's just kid stuff. They will be over it tomorrow."

Yeah, Mom didn't have to listen to stories about a freak dad with no legs! No one was teasing my mother! I was just hanging there as if I was luggage. I quit fighting. The bus driver set me down and now my mother grabs my arm before he lets go of me. It hurts! They said goodbye and she apologized to him again. I thought my arm was bleeding where she dug in her fingernails and I told her she was hurting me.

"Shut up." She shook me a little as we walked into the yard and inside the house. She told me it was wrong to fist fight. She told me girls didn't act like that. She made me weary, at the ripe age of eleven, of hearing what girls couldn't do. I wanted to be a boy; they got to fight. They didn't have to do so many chores and they didn't have to wear dresses!

She was telling me it was okay to stick up for my father; however, it was not okay to get into fights.

I wasn't sticking up for him; I was embarrassed and furious about the abomination that would be my father.

Didn't they hear me? Doesn't anybody ever hear me?

I didn't understand why we had to move. I liked it here in the trailer park. I didn't want to move. I didn't want to go see my father in the hospital. How could anyone live without their body parts? My mom threw away my stuffed monkey because the arm was coming off. "No good without his arm," she had said and into the dumpster it went.

I had loved that toy more than anything. Tearfully I told her, "I love my monkey."

She slapped me. "Stop that, you are not a baby anymore. We don't keep broken things."

But, Daddy is broken and we have to keep him? I was confused.

We left for the naval hospital in California. No more bay. There would be no more fishing, crabbing or looking for bottles to take in for pennies at the old store. We were going to California. I guess that was where they sent people who lose body parts in explosions. I kept thinking about a movie I saw when I snuck out of bed in the middle of the night – there were people walking around with no heads, and they were in California.

We arrived before our mobile home did and stayed for quite a while in a motel room.

To kill time, we often went to the zoo. The monkey was a favorite of ours. He spat water at us and we thought this was funny. We spat water back at the cage. Mother would say, "That is not funny," though she did laugh on occasion.

The monkey began to spit back more efficiently than we did. He could spit mouthfuls of water and was a better shot. My mother told us several times that it was mean to spit water like that, but we laugh and tell her in unison, "He likes it!"

As she began to admonish us with one of her lectures, she suddenly got soaked. She was gasping! She was horrified! She was quite wet!

"This is not funny!" Then she sputters, "We are leaving." She grabs my younger brothers' hands and marches toward the gate and out to the parking area.

John and I were laughing hysterically. My stomach hurt from laughing. We had to go back to the motel so Mother could change into dry clothes, because later that day we were going to see our father for the first time. Mother wants to look nice; she wants us to look nice.

I wanted to look ugly. I would have rather seen the monkey spitting water again.

When we got to the hospital, we went through the familiar guard gates of a military base. I was used to that. I could see many long white buildings; I saw them as barracks, but would learn later that it was a hospital and the wards were filled with injured soldiers, most of them casualties from Vietnam.

I was still in denial about my father's injuries. All of this trip was somewhat familiar, since I'd been on and off military bases my whole life. How could something so horrible be waiting for us inside one of those familiar buildings?

As she pulled the car into a parking space, Mom began a lecture, telling us to behave ourselves as we got out of the car. Satisfied that she scared us into behaving, we walked up a hill to one of the white buildings. There was a ramp instead of stairs for us to walk up into the building. We went through double doors that led into a sunny solarium filled with several uncomfortable chairs, one small sofa and three soda machines. There were ashtrays on both ends of the seating arrangement. Windows on all three sides let in a lot of light. It was warm, almost hot, in the afternoon sun. Black and white industrial linoleum squares made a checkerboard on the floor. We moved into the center of this waiting room. To the left was another set of wide double doors. These had been left open and led into a long, open, ward with beds lining the walls on both sides. The ward of people with missing body parts.

When Daddy got his appendix out we were not allowed in. We were supposed to feel bad for him and take care of him, but kids couldn't go to the hospital because they were dirty and would make people sick and get them infected. He came out to see us in a visitor yard.

I got my tonsils out in a hospital, but I only remembered toys, ice cream and my mom being angry that it didn't hurt me. She got her tonsils out at the same time and apparently suffered a lot.

"The nurses' station is at the other end of this ward," Mom said, interrupting my thoughts. "I want you to behave yourselves, no fighting, no talking, no running around."

But, to get there...I have to take a breath!

She didn't tell us what we would see. There were a hundred guys in there! They were everywhere with missing arms, legs, eyes, and skin burned off to the bone. There were mangled fingers at the end of twisted arms. There were faces that look like they were melted and one guy appeared to be missing his jaw. A guy over there was missing an arm, leg and eye, all on his left side. I tried to tell my mother to look, but she kept pushing me. Another guy smiled, waving a hook where a hand should be as we entered. He winked at me with his one good eye and the scarred side of his face wrinkled in an odd way. It was almost as if he tried to blink at me, but the missing eye was confused.

The next bed had a young guy drinking out of a cologne bottle. I shouldn't have stared. It was rude. I didn't want to be rude, but I couldn't help it. There was so much to look at and I didn't know what to think about it all. Should I have waved back? Should I have looked at the floor? Should I pretend they were all normal? In the end, I was rude. I stared. I had to stare – I just couldn't help it.

My mother kept pushing me. "Don't dawdle, you aren't really supposed to be in here!" Another shove. "Don't you want to see your father?"

I didn't answer as I saw disfigured man after disfigured man. I didn't want to be there. I didn't particularly care if I saw my father. I didn't want to see any of this! My frustration was physical. I wanted her to stop touching me and stop pushing me. She kept pushing on my shoulder to herd me forward. I wanted her to wake me up. I wanted her to take me out of there. My stomach hurt and I burned where she touched my back. I thought, if she pushes me one more time I will jump out a window! My head is pounding in frustration as I tried to comprehend what I was seeing.

I was unable to take anymore and I turned to her, hissing, "Quit pushing me!"

My mother replied, "Get that chip off your shoulder, young lady. People went to a lot of trouble to let you in here. Don't you want to see your father?"

NO! I am screaming in my head where no one can hear it. I would be ignored if I said it aloud and then I would be slapped for sure. I did not want to see any of this!

Of course my answer has to be yes. I knew that I was supposed to say I wanted to see him. I didn't. I didn't want to see any more of this, but I kept my mouth shut and I saw more. It was one shock to my senses after another.

Why were they making us do this? Some were badly burned; all were missing something that I thought you needed to live. That guy over there had no arms at all and was crying. As the weeks wore on, I would find out that he cried most of the time. He was supposed to get married and his fiancé left him when this happened. His heart is broken; I knew that even at my young age.

The closer we got to the nurses' station the worse it was: moaning, crying, and some of them just lying there – seemingly dead. Later I would find out that those closest to the nurses' station were not dead, just drugged heavily. They were the latest victims of the Vietnam War.

As new patients were shipped in, the older ones were pushed down the squad bay symbolically towards the door. However, that day I didn't know about drugs for pain or alcohol snuck into after-shave bottles to drink away the horror of their new bodies and the new lives they didn't ask for. That day, they all just look like zombies: white, bloody, beat up and barely breathing.

It would be twenty years before it occurred to anyone that families in this situation needed counseling. Back then, no one in my family could have risked that sort of exposure, anyway. We had too much to hide already.

Finally, we came to my father. His bed was stationed right in front of the nurses' window. He looked dead. He had no color, was very thin, and his dark hair was greasy. He just lay there. I looked for his feet. I looked for a bent leg. The white sheet lays flat. It was true! His left leg was gone from the hip and it looked like he might have part of a right leg under there. He was in a huge bed with the sides up. The bed was tall; it was even with my shoulder. The nurses have drawn the curtain and I can't see them. My mother instructs us, "Stay with your father."

I'm speechless! She went to let the nurses know we were all there. Stay here?

John went to the opposite side of the bed for a better look at that missing leg. Gabe was ready to cry, so Mom picked him up and took him with her around the corner. I was glad, because I didn't know what to say to him. Poor Gabe, he was probably crying at the scary zombie movie we were in.

I continued to stare at the flat spot on the bed where the rest of Daddy's body should have been. There really were no legs! Dad looked skinny, white and helpless. I was speechless. My dad – helpless?

He turned his head slowly to my brother John. "Hey, big guy." His voice was barely above a whisper.

John smiled from ear to ear. I didn't hear what else Dad said to him. His face was turned away from me. John looked at me and smiled as Dad weakly touched his face. He dropped his hand back to the bed, clearly tired from the effort.

He slowly turned to me now, again, with effort. He focused on me and smiled weakly. I tried to smile back. I didn't know what to say, but I had say something! It was my dad lying there. I smiled as Mom told us to and said, "Hi Daddy."

He smiled and said so softly that John couldn't hear: "Hi punkin, can you give me a blow job before your mother comes back? It would only take a minute. Daddy missed you."

I could only stand there staring at him. I am not shocked at his request. I'd heard it before and in an odd way, it confirms for me that this really is my father. I don't answer. He doesn't seem to care. He seems to fade off and I wasn't sure, but I think he went to sleep.

It's too white. The walls are white. The linen is white. All the maimed and blown-up men are wearing white pajamas. Their skin is white, their eyes sunken into thin faces. My brothers apparently know how to behave. They are jumping up and down happy to see him now that they see he is awake. I stand mute, staring, thinking over his greeting, wondering why God would have saved him. There must not be a God after all. He looks bad, maybe he will still die.

Oh God, I hope so.

God's Country

ABOUT A YEAR AFTER THAT first day at the hospital, several of the patients were taken on a hunting and camping trip by some group hoping to show them that life went on. Daddy went on that trip, and came home and announced that we were moving. He said he discovered God's country. Property was bought, a house built and we were leaving soon. So, again, the old mobile home is relocated. My mother was told it wouldn't have to go through another move. "I don't expect to be moving again," she smiles.

When the trailer arrived on the property in northern California, they parked it next to an old house that sat on the ten acres that was now ours. There was a water pump in the front yard and I was completely enamored with it. It was pretty there.

We slept on the floor of the old house that first night, since we had arrived before the mobile home did. We were lined up in sleeping bags and blankets in a row on the floor in what would be the living room: John, Gabe, my mother, then me, then my father. I was sandwiched between my parents – one hates me and the other can't keep his hands off me. I said I wanted to sleep by John and Gabe but I was admonished by my mother, "Just do as you are told for once!"

John and Gabe settled in to sleep. I lay there faking sleep. I heard my mother's even breathing as she fell asleep.

My father nudged me persistently.

Finally, he hissed at me, "I know you are not asleep."

I stiffen.

"Do it or I will wake her up and tell her to beat you black and bloody. She lives to beat the crap out of you little bastards!"

I complied, with all my brothers in the room, and right next to my mother, who never moved. What amazing control he had over me. He knew I wouldn't ask her for help. I was convinced she wouldn't give it to me anyway.

MOM AND DAD planned to build a house and were talking to architects all the time and poring over blueprints. There was money from the government for the extra expense to make it wheelchair accessible.

While the construction was going on, we lived in the mobile home. A veteran's group came out and built a redwood deck and a ramp leading down to the old house that Dad would use for a workshop. The ramp led down to a back door. That back door appeared to open into a bedroom; I say that because there was another door in the other wall that led directly into the kitchen area. All this turned out to be handy for Dad. He could zip in and out in his wheelchair all he wanted. He couldn't get back up the ramp on his own though. He would scream in frustration for someone to, "Get your goddamn lazy fucking ass down here and get me!" One of us would be off and running to get him.

In the beginning, we felt a little sorry for him. We had some empathy. Even as children, in our own naive, unsophisticated way, we knew this had to be a terrible thing to live with. We did try to understand and help, but it was never enough. It would become about Dad only. His wants, his needs, his desires and ultimately his fantasies, were all that mattered.

He used the old house as type of solitary confinement for us.

When I was in eighth grade, my father grounded me and sent me to that room in the old house for two weeks – I didn't leave it during the entire time. John told me years later he was sure it had been much longer. I didn't recall. Dad could visit whenever he wanted and it was private. He would nail the doors shut; there were no windows.

I wished that old house would burn to the ground. He used it to work on projects, like his unsuccessful venture in raising chinchillas. He'd shoot himself up with Demerol and putter around as if he was really doing something. On occasion, he would produce a work of art. When that happened, one could see a glimmer of who he could have been if he had a shred of ambition; he just didn't have the commitment it took to see something through to completion.

My father would take twenty or thirty single dollar bills and wrap a $50 or $100 bill around the whole thing to make it look like he had a lot of money. The perception of who he appeared to be was so important to him. It was too much work to live a life that mattered. If it wasn't easy, he wasn't interested. He was a compulsive liar. He once told me, "I'm a cripple and a war hero; they won't dare call me a liar."

He owned an art shop for a while. He made redwood burls into slab coffee tables and end tables. He had some very nice pieces and folks would come in to look if he happened to be open. He was rarely open. He had a sign on the door that set his hours: "When I'm in and if you catch me."

Eventually, he used it only as a front for his drug-related activities and the women he was somehow always able to find, attract and have sex with. He had to have sex with everyone and everything. It reminded me of a dog humping the leg of a chair.

He learned to do things in spite of his disability. He learned to ski – not because he was a skier before his legs were blown off, but because there was a program offering free lessons and he felt he had something to prove. He never did it again. Soon he discovered, he didn't really have to accomplish anything. He just had to talk about it and it was so. He was right. No one would ever call a him a liar.

I remember when he was stopped for speeding. When he saw the red lights coming for him as he sped down the road, he released the belt that held on his prosthetic leg and the fell onto the floor. When the officer came up to the window, he opened the door and turned in the seat to show his disability and therefore, his lack of culpability. To my knowledge, this worked every time. The pity card got him out of so many violations. He delighted in telling me and others that they would never send him to prison since it would cost them too much to keep him there. Somehow, his disability gave him permission to behave as he pleased.

I watched him once in a grocery store as he sat in his wheelchair talking to a little boy about four years old. He was a cute little kid with dark hair and big eyes that looked bigger as he stared at my father.

"What happened to your legs?" the boy asked, barely above a whisper.

"My legs?" says my dad. "My cat ate them!"

That poor little boy visibly paled as he replied, "I have a cat."

Dad was getting ready to answer that when the little boy's mother came over and whisked him off telling him it wasn't polite to stare and ask questions.

Someone should have chastised my father about what was polite and what wasn't.

He called the mother of that kid a stupid cunt and said she was a phony bitch to drag the kid off; said she wanted to stare too. Maybe she did. God knows I did plenty of staring the year he was in the hospital. Even though I lost that horror-show feeling, I never lost the incredulity of knowing those men had to live like that and I always wondered how they did it.

My father was thirty-three when he was in the explosion that cost him his legs. I always knew he was the same height as my mother, 5'7"; he was an insecure man before the accident and the loss of his legs made him more so. Sixteen years after I was born, my mother had another baby boy – Bryan, named after my father. Looking back, I think it was because my father wanted to prove that he could. I'm not sure my mother wanted another baby, but my father's ego won out.

As the years went by, my brothers grew, and so did my father – to well over six feet. He had back issues because of it. The pegs he used as artificial legs got longer and longer with every passing year.

I asked him why he was making himself taller.

He answered, "This is how tall I am really supposed to be. I just had short legs. God's error."

"Imagine that," I thought. "God's error."

The Burning Bed

WHEN I WAS SIXTEEN, DAD went to see a gypsy woman. She read his tarot cards, his palms, my palms, tea leaves, burnt hair and candle drippings. These were all just the tip of the iceberg concerning her talents – she did it all. He would break out the wad of one-dollar bills wrapped in a hundred-dollar bill. This seemed to magnify her mystical talent for telling the future and fixing all ills.

I guess she told him to bring me and then to bring Mom. So, after school one afternoon, he took me to see her. The place looked like a warehouse with creepy, dirty-looking offices. A few had signs on their doors. The gypsy woman's door did not. Dad commented that he thought she lived there.

That day my father added a couple of twenties to his roll. She required payment in advance for her services. When he took the cash out of his pocket she eyed the great wad. Smiling broadly, she hugged him and told him how much she missed him that week. She then exclaimed breathlessly, "I have much to tell you..."

She must see his hands and read his cards right away. He agrees and she starts telling the future before the cards are out on the table.

He says to me, "She is amazing! I wanted you to see how good she is."

It appears that my father, the con man, has been completely conned! It's mind-bending to watch as he peels off the money to give to this woman. He has begun making decisions about his life based on what she tells him.

She tells me how happy she is to finally see me as she beckons me over to a door. As she opens it, she has to push a curtain out of the way for us to enter. The closet-sized room is creepy: there are black curtains all around, dim lights and black and red lace hangs everywhere.

I'm sitting at a small round table with candles burning off to the side. And there it is; the crystal ball. The whole scene is straight out of a "Dracula" film.

I try to hand her the money that Dad gave me to pay her.

"I can't take money – no money from you," she says in a thick accent.

"What? Why?" I feel blank. Everybody takes money. I am confused and tell her, "I am supposed to give you this money!"

"No, no money for your reading, God look out for you. You have white aura! Can't take no money from you."

I am sure my dad is going to be angry about this. I want to leave. "He said to give you this money!" I say, feeling the panic rising in my chest.

She stands up and with some effort, heaves her short, round body around the table and I follow. I do not intend to be trapped in her dark, curtained, tiny room. I blink as we enter the waiting area as the sun blazes into the room.

She marches over to Dad and tells him, "I don't take no money for her. Not allowed."

The hook is set.

After this, he makes no decisions without consulting her cards, burning her candles, or whatever other suggestion she has for making his life better. These remedies don't come cheap.

"If she was a fake, she would take my cash," he assures me.

I think it's a little creepy, but then again, I am jaded. She is an adult. Adults lie, cheat and prey upon one another.

The gypsy woman came to our house often. She was being consulted about the 'haunting' some members of my family are experiencing, and about my behavior: I was constantly accused of hiding knives between my mattress and the box spring. I insisted that I hadn't put them there. My mother sees hands in the sink washing dishes. Heavy wall hangings find their way off the wall and onto the floor across the room with no-one ever hearing anything. Cold spots in a room, rearranged furniture, and according to my mother, the smell of roses in my bedroom. All this is the cause of great alarm for the gypsy woman.

We had to perform ceremonies since the bad spirits were after me. I was being possessed by a poltergeist.

One of these ceremonies is in full swing when I get home from school one sunny afternoon. Out in the back yard, while my father sits in his wheelchair watching, the gypsy and my mother are circling my bed.

"WHAT?! My bed is in the back yard! What are you doing?"

The two women stop, startled by my unexpected appearance. They each have cans of coffee in their hands and are circling my bed sprinkling the grounds around it.

My mother starts to tell me, "We are…" Her voice falters.

The gypsy woman says with great confidence, "We burn bed! Exorcise evil from your room."

I just stare at them. I'm told I have somehow invited the Devil's creatures into my family. They must perform this ritual to rid us of them. I continue to look on, too mystified to be angry.

Am I the bad one? Maybe they are right.

Suddenly the bed is burning and the gypsy is chanting some gibberish I can't understand. I back up as it bursts into flames. A fireball explodes and black smoke rolls out. The gypsy exclaims, "That is evil spirit!"

I wonder about the basic fire safety we've been taught about gasoline and other chemicals in school this year. I make the mistake of asking if they threw gasoline on the bed to make it burn that way.

"The devil is in you! He is making you ask those questions!" The gypsy woman says angrily. "We think you don't want to get rid of the Devil. We will exorcise him from you and from this house!"

They are all looking at me oddly. Suddenly, it occurs to me that they might set me on fire. I decide to leave.

"I gotta go – I'm going to be late for work." I tell them. I shake my head to myself as I get into the car and drive away to the restaurant where I work.

When I came home, the bed was gone. It had been burned to ashes and as I gazed upon the mess left behind, I thought that this was a testament to the insanity of life on this ten-acre hobby farm.

My parents were in bed. Now what? I wondered for a moment where to sleep. I took a blanket and pillow and went to the sofa. It's just another day in my week. It doesn't even keep me awake. 'Hey, my father didn't get my paycheck today,' I laughed to myself. He was so busy burning my bed that he forgot to go down and snag it from my boss.

My father always went and took my paycheck on payday. I never saw any of that money. If I wanted money, I had to hide the tips I got working as a waitress.

Later, with my windfall money, I went and bought a waterbed from a hippie who had opened up a shop downtown. It cost me one hundred dollars. There was no heater. All I had was the frame and the waterbed mattress but it beat the sofa and the floor.

Apparently, I was still possessed – even with my new bed. There was, however, no place for them to look and find a knife; no one can crawl under the waterbed.

Maybe this situation had turned out well, after all.

Pushing Back

I'M IN THE KITCHEN FINISHING chores, hoping to run off with friends when I'm done. Mom is at the dining table with her friend. Their talk is about psychics, the gypsy woman, séances, automatic handwriting, and whatever weird thing no one else can see. It's creepy and I hate it. I don't want to hear about Ouija boards, ghosts or body parts in or near the sink. I don't want to hear about bodies, primarily mine, being possessed. They have decided that I am without a doubt possessed by some evil spirit. Being possessed makes me the cause of anything and everything wrong in this house. This includes the well going dry, as it has on a daily basis since we moved in, hot water running out, my brother missing the bus or my mother having a headache.

LET ME OUT OF HERE!

My mother is still talking about the hands she sees in the sink when no one else is home. Just hands washing dishes in the sink; not washing our dishes mind you, but washing someone else's. She hears voices, too. I don't know what the voices say. I don't want to know either, I can tell you that! It scares the hell out of me when they start talking about this crap when it's dark outside. However, right now it's early Saturday afternoon and I want to hurry up and get the kitchen done so I can get out of this place. Mom believes she is telepathic. Such bullshit! You didn't see Dad with that girl who lives down the street, did you? Oh yeah, the Telepathic Gods must block the stuff he does to me, too.

I'm in a hurry to get moving. I'm not grounded and before my situation changes I would like to get out of here. Listening to them is annoying and slowing me down. I don't often get the chance to get out on my own and I am sure as hell not sticking around today.

Wait, WHAT?

I stand absolutely still and listen so hard that it makes my head hurt.

Did I hear that right?

Push…back? I am reeling with the idea. This is profound. OH! MY! GOD! It's so simple. Push back! Are you kidding me? Did I hear that right?

I'm thunderstruck with the thought. I can't believe I am hearing it. This came from the same woman who dragged me kicking and screaming over to my father in the past. Her reason for it was that it would just be worse when he caught me later.

My mother never stopped him from beating us. My father did whatever he felt like and we all played his game.

There my mother sits, at our kitchen table, telling another woman, "One of these days, one of those kids is going to wise up. They're going to realize that he's a cripple in that chair and they're going to push back."

I can hear my mother's voice in my head for days as if she's just said it. It's a profound moment in my life.

I am and have always been terrified of my father. Always. After the loss of his legs, he was worse. The demons in his head got bigger and braver with every swindle or con he got away with until he believed even God would not punish him.

"God," he would say, "is here for me, not you." I believed him.

We are beaten until we have trouble getting up. We have tables thrown over on us at dinner. We are dragged out of bed in the middle of the night, beaten, and tossed around our room or the rest of the house. My father's arms were huge and he was strong from the crutches and wheelchairs. Once in his grip there was no escape. I've been stabbed with knives, forks and ice picks. I've been beaten with a bullwhip, sticks, his fist, or anything else he had handy, including his fake leg. He once had left it leaning up against the wall and while pounding on me with his fist, he was close enough to pick up the leg. It was surreal to see a shoe attached to a leg coming at me from over my head like a baseball bat.

All my father had to say was, "Get your ass over here."

I did just that. I walk right over, stand there, let him grab me by the arm, and beat me with his other fist. It simply does not occur to John or me to run away or simply stay out of his reach and out of danger.

My brother Gabe tried. On that occasion, John and Dad tied his arms to a broomstick handle and beat him for running away.

Yes, John beat his own brother – but before you judge him, understand that he was only a kid and the beating he would get from Dad for not doing it would have been life threatening. Another time Gabe ran away from Dad, managing to elude him for a few days. When Dad finally caught up to him, he stapled Gabe to the floor of the old house I had been trapped in, beat him badly, and urinated on him.

We were well trained; we did as we were told and we never ran away from Daddy. He told us with a most sympathetic voice, "You have to take your medicine now, or later it will taste a lot worse. It's for your own good," he would sigh.

"It hurts me worse than it hurts you," he would say sadly. "I don't know why you make me do this to you."

I never thought about how to make him stop. It never occurred to me to push back. I never comprehended that he might have become vulnerable. For my entire life he had been the meanest man I ever knew. I lived because he allowed me to. He would tell me what to think and when to think it. He brought me into the world, therefore I owed him. He owned me. He could do whatever he wanted to me. He was my father. He was my God. I never thought of hitting him back.

It was a profoundly simple thought: Push him back.

I can't remember any other part of the conversation my mother had with her friend that day. However, that one sentence was a turning point in my life. It echoed in my head repeatedly at oddest of times.

In the middle of algebra, which I was failing. "One of these days…"

In the middle of U.S. History, which I needed to pass to graduate. "…push him back."

Art class was the only place I could be free of crazy thoughts, free to lose myself in the moment, fearlessly creating my own world. I loved painting, drawing, and sculpting. I loved making things.

I hate taking them home.

After the "That's nice," my work of art became kindling. Why did he always throw my stuff out when he got his hands on it?

"All that time and work. Forget about it! It doesn't matter! It's just gone now and it doesn't matter," I told myself. "I will graduate and I will move away. Soon I will move away. Soon I will be grown up."

In the meantime… pills and pot. They were just enough to make me not care what he did, or the nothing my mother did.

The nothing she did as she sat in the corner with her cigarettes, wine, and fat, bright red, lips.

Knowing

IT'S A BEAUTIFUL DAY TODAY and I enjoyed the walk home from the bus. The azaleas are in bloom and they smell wonderful. The sun feels good on my skin. I smoke some weed on the way home in preparation for an evening with my family.

I see Daddy in the kitchen as I come through the door. The kitchen is just off the dining area and it's big, with counters low enough for Daddy. There are many windows to let in the sun. It's a nice house. The dining table accommodates eight to ten people easily. A brick fireplace separates the kitchen from the living room. The whole house is built to accommodate my father's wheelchair; all the rooms are larger, with wider doorways and hallways.

I muse that no one will ever believe the shit that goes on around here.

I waste a couple of seconds of my thoughts on "if" – if anyone knew. Can you imagine what the kids at school would do if they knew? No one would ever talk to me again. It would be bad, very bad.

Daddy is in the kitchen banging pots around. He seems to be in an okay mood. He does all the cooking and is in the kitchen getting ready to make dinner. He sees himself as a gourmet cook. Grudgingly, I have to admit he can cook. I wonder foggily what he is cooking tonight. In my pot-induced haze I almost giggle aloud as I wondered if it will end up on the floor as dog food. I wonder if he will lose his temper over some bullshit thing and dump the table over. Maybe he will just throw some of that food around the room while I am in the bathroom eating.

I don't want to think about that anymore. It's ruining my high.

I am mulling these thoughts over and marveling at my peaceful mood. I smile to myself; I don't have many days like this. It's been a good day. I played tennis at school and won again. I am going to try out for cheerleader with a couple of friends. My art teacher told me I had done some good ink work. Maybe I could tell Mom and Dad about my day. I chuckle to myself.

He is screaming at me about something.

"What? I just got home!"

I've been here five minutes, minding my own business and he is screaming at me already. I'm just sitting here! He is mad about a greasy dish or a dirty knife left in the sink.

I hate this house; the shallow well goes dry with a single sink-full of water. It doesn't even run enough water to get hot. These water issues make it difficult to wash dishes and do laundry. Taking a bath is a trial and showers are out of the question. I'm not allowed to leave the kitchen until the dishes are done. This makes for a lose-lose situation. If it takes too long, it makes my parents angry; if I get them done fast, they aren't clean.

How the fuck do you wash dinner dishes for six people with cold water?

"Don't swear," I hear my own voice in my head, "it makes you sound like him!"

Daddy, though good at making meals, is a messy cook. He uses every pot he can find, and doesn't bother to rinse as he goes. By the time dinner is over, the food is cemented to pots, bowls, plates, utensils and every other thing he touched. This happens every day.

He is screaming at me and calling me names. "Get your fat, fucking ass over here!"

This means a visit to my room tonight for sure. I don't care. I'll smoke more weed or take some pills, maybe both. There is Demerol in the master bathroom. However, I will think about it later, because right now I am walking over to stand in front of him.

As I slowly make my way over to him, he is screaming about what a superior human he is.

"I am your God! You exist because I allow it! If I say shit, you ask me how much and what color! You lazy little cunt, I want those dishes clean!"

The raging goes on: I am nothing but garbage, trash, a maggot, a piece of shit and a whore.

He is fading. I am standing in front of him and marveling that I am not afraid. I'm disconnected and strangely calm. 'Must have been some awful good pot,' I think to myself.

For the first time it's interesting that his face is red and he is sweating as he screams. Sweating? Who sweats because they are yelling at a kid?

I think he asked me something, but all I can do is blink.

I keep staring, studying him as if he were a bug I've never seen before. I feel blurred and a little formless as I hear my mother's voice, "One of these days, one of these days, one of these days . . ."

I feel a caught between the tilting grayness and the present. It must be the pot. I can't really hear him. There is a rush in my ears like running water and the pressure behind my eyes is tremendous. Then very clearly, I hear a voice in the back of my head, "Push him back!"

It's not my mother's voice. Who is that?

"Push him back! Push him! PUSH HIM! BACK! PUSH BACK! PUSH! PUSH! PUSH!"

It doesn't sound like a real word anymore. It's a frenzied voice screaming at me, "DO IT!"

I'm not responding the way he expects me to, and so he is getting visibly angrier: screaming, spitting and cursing. I can see it coming. He is going to beat me, but I feel oddly disconnected and I don't care. I think again that it must be the pot. Suddenly, he whips his arm out and there is instant white-hot pain. He stabbed me in the elbow!

He's been waving that little paring knife around like a baton, punctuating whatever was spewing out of his mouth. I stupidly ignored it. It appeared too small to do any damage, and so I dismissed it.

"Goddamn!" I scream.

He stabbed me with that skinny little knife he has in his hand. Blood sprayed out. I suddenly remember the fork he stuck in my thigh last summer. The shock of the knife sticking in my arm was too much. He was going to kill me, damn it! He was going to stab me to death with forks, knives, bullwhips and fucking feet that leaned up against the wall! I was going to die from whatever weird thing he had in his hand. Can you be killed with eating utensils? Could he beat me to death with his leg? I am one step away from laughing at the absurdity of it all. I am also hot with anger and at the same time, numb.

There is a lot of blood but I don't care about it anymore. The pain stops suddenly as if a switch is turned off. All I care about was this asshole killing me with that goddamn little knife! I could see myself being pierced and pricked repeatedly until I look like Swiss cheese.

It's not the first time I've been stabbed with something he had in his hand, but I have decided from a place inside of myself that I've never gone to before that it will be the last time. I won't be stuck with a knife, fork or ice pick again. I won't be beaten like this again. He is not going to kill me. I am not going to wait for him to kill me. I am not going to let him touch me one more time while my flesh crawls.

He is standing on his peg-legs now with his wheel chair behind him for balance. He does this often when getting ready to grab me for a serious beating. A slap in the face or a heel of the hand to the forehead causes raging headaches but makes no marks, and it can all be done sitting down. A real beating requires getting up.

I feel vaguely disconnected but aware of my situation. I've been stabbed and now he is punching me. I reel backwards twisting my arm and breaking his hold on me and hear the voice again.

"One of these days, one of those kids is going to push back."

I hear it again, "One of these days, one of those kids are going to push back."

It is surely not my mother's voice...

"One of these days, one of these days, one of these days!"

TODAY! PUSH HIM!

I shoot out both of my hands and lunge forward, hitting him in the chest. It is a solid hit. He doesn't see it coming. His mouth falls open in shock as he slams back into his chair. The brake is on and he lands hard in the seat. He now releases it and comes after me. As he gets up, I shove him back before he has his balance. I push harder this time as I begin to feel empowered. This time he reels violently backward into his chair. Without the brakes on, he rolls back into the kitchen. He is incensed.

I've been given permission. I can still hear the screaming, "PUSH! PUSH! PUSH!"

Daddy is screaming at me, calling me names. My mother is in my head again screaming at me to hit him; he is screaming that he is going to kill me. Where is my mother? I briefly look around. Where is she? How come I can hear her? Why can't I see her? I am momentarily distracted and he hits me again.

I don't have time to think about it. I've set something in motion and it's too late to stop. Now it is preservation. I know if I stop now, he will kill me. I am now without conscience. There is no consequence I can think of, I have to make him leave me alone. The screaming and spitting rages will stop. The confusion will stop. The never-ending false accusations will stop. He won't hit me again, or stab me again, nope . . . and he won't be visiting my room tonight.

I saw it when I came in.

There on the dining table, loaded, no locks, no safety, just waiting for me like a gift, was one of Daddy's own shotguns. I've been shooting guns with my father since I was very young. It was commonplace for guns to be lying around the house. It made him feel like more of a man, to brag about his ownership of so many guns and his superhuman marksmanship.

Not taking my eyes off him as I back away, I see his confusion. I've never backed away before. I come around the table and pick up the shotgun. In one swift smooth motion, I check it, cock it, and very calmly stick it in his face. I have no panic. I am calm. My heart is still. I like it.

Suddenly, he looks a little gray.

I smile.

The sound of the shotgun bolt sliding is deeply satisfying. It's a terrifying sound to the person unlucky enough to be looking down the barrel and realizing there is no missing ten inches away from your face. I know this is true. He's done it to me more than once to prove his power and control over me. He used us for target practice with his high-powered BB gun. I thought about that briefly . . .

My brother and I run across the yard as he laughs and shoots at us.

"Be still!" he would yell. "I don't need to practice on a moving target."

Not so funny now is it, you bastard!

I ponder a thought for a moment. Maybe I can make him wheel around the room in his chair and make pig noises. I briefly envision him oinking and snorting. Nah – that'll take too long.

For the first time in my sixteen years of life, the man who brought me into the world, the man who is my God, who allows me to live, who tells me what to think and when to think it, has shut his big . . . fat . . . mouth. Now he is the one who is afraid while I allow him to live for a moment more.

I don't know what he sees in my face and I give it little, if any, thought. In my mind, I have already pulled the trigger.

I blow his head right off his shoulders.

The bone splinters and blood splatters as the shotgun rebounds in my hands. In slow motion, I see the blood and brain matter blow through the air onto the kitchen window, the cupboards, the sink, and the kitchen counter. I watch with satisfaction as chunks of his head drip down the kitchen walls and the ceiling. Fragments of bone and brain stick to the walls in macabre patterns. There is blood spurting from his neck, where his head used to be, much as it had spurted from the chickens we beheaded. I see all this gore. I don't care. I smile to myself as I hear him babbling at me.

He is talking calmly to me. "Daddy's sorry. Daddy didn't mean to lose his temper."

I am not listening. I don't care what he is saying. His lips are moving. So what! He's sorry?

I am bleeding where he stuck me with a goddamned knife!

I have a scar from the ice pick and a fork mark on my thigh!

I have a damn cigarette burn on my forehead!

What's next? A bigger knife? A bigger fork?

Nope, no next time for me.

The sadistic bastard probably dreams up the shit he does to us while he sleeps. In a moment, I will stop those lips from moving. He is afraid and I am enjoying the moment. I smile, nearly laughing aloud with the giddiness of the feeling. This afternoon, this moment, I have the power. I am his God. I am allowing him to live for one more minute because, I am enjoying it. This is my moment.

He will never bother me again.

He will never hit me again.

He will never visit me again.

He will never give me to his friends or some boy from school.

I haven't had to say a word. He knows I will do it. He knows he deserves it. He is sitting in his wheelchair looking at that gun in his ashen face. He is afraid. He can smell death coming for him. Victory! I shift my finger onto the trigger in anticipation.

The gun is wrenched out of my hands.

Nobody else is home! I whirl around.

"What the hell?"

My brother John has appeared from nowhere. The shotgun is in his hands now. He has released the shells and thrown them on the table. Now my father is triumphant. How quickly the hands of power can change, in just the blink of an eye.

Dad is calling me names and screaming at me again. My mother shows up wanting to know what is going on. Where did she come from? Where has she been all this time?

She was just screaming, "Push, push!" wasn't she?

Why does she always show up when I look like the bad one? She is screaming. It all happened in a split second.

Dad is telling my mother, "She was trying to kill me!" He is righteous and pointing at the gun. "I'm a crippled man!"

My mother is hitting me for trying to kill him. Dad has hold of my arm while he is screaming, calling me names and telling me to get out at his house. Suddenly, he let go, "You are too disgusting to waste my fucking energy on," he says. My brother looks confused and is backing out of the room. He did his part and now that all hell is breaking loose, he is wise to get the hell out.

Mom is yelling at me, "Get out of my house. I don't want you living here anymore. What's the matter with you?"

Fine! I don't want to live here.

I am leaving with the clothes I am wearing. I can sneak back into my room and get the stuff I need later tonight. Mom will drink a gallon of wine and Dad will be crashed out on Demerol. They won't even know I'm here.

I must have rattled him good. I don't care. He isn't hitting me. I would expect he would beat me within an inch of my life for that sort of disrespect. He could have.

I left.

I AM FURIOUS with my brother for months.

John had been coming home from school, and as he passed the dining room window, he saw what was going on inside. He was stunned by what he was witnessing. He was sure I meant to finish Dad off. John told me later, "It would have been suicide not to pull the trigger once you picked it up and stuck it in his face."

He ran around the house and snuck in through the back bedroom window. He came in behind me and wrenched the shotgun out of my hands, and I never heard him coming.

I was so focused on terrorizing Daddy and reveling in the power I had, I lost my chance. Another thirty seconds, life would have been changed forever for everyone. My father lived another thirty years because he had enough common sense to be afraid that day.

Most people don't live with the knowledge that they are capable of slaughtering another human being. I know I am. I know I would have.

I wish I didn't have that knowledge.

Moving Out

"YOU ARE HORMONE DEFICIENT." MY mother explains, "This is causing you to not grow properly." My parents would yank my hair and leave me with bald spots. When I was cleaning up the turned over furniture from sessions, I would find strands of hair. I was too traumatized at the time to realize it was mine. When I would later brush my hair, fistfuls would be left in the brush. They told me I was losing my hair because I didn't eat enough. I believed them. Denial is something that can save your sanity. According to Dad, I was little for the same reason. My brothers ate like horses and were big, tall boys. I believed everything they told me. He piled food on my plate that I couldn't eat. Often I was sick after family meals.

I don't care. I don't want to grow up. Besides, how does she even notice whether I am growing? I have already had a lifetime of hearing what it is going to be like to be grown up. I am not in any hurry.

I am also not menstruating and it is an obsession with my father. I am shared with his friends as well, grown men with their own daughters. Boys my age are often in my bedroom, by my father's invitation. He is taking me to see the doctor for birth control pills. I'm sure; quite sure, pregnancy is becoming a concern.

The day arrives.

Dad tells me as we drive to the doctor's office there is no need to worry about this, it will be fine. He assures me he has already talked to the doctor and everything is taken care of. I have no idea what to expect or what to ask. By the time we arrive, I understand I am to say nothing.

Dad never leaves me alone with the doctor, nor does the doctor ask me any questions. The doctor doesn't even ask why I needed to be on the pill.

While lying on a table with my feet in the stirrups feeling violated, they discuss what a modern father he is and how more fathers should be like him. No one is concerned about my embarrassment and humiliation while my father sits in the room for the exam. Not one question was asked of me during this appointment. Only Daddy answered questions. Afterward, he brags for weeks about the doctor who praised him for being a progressive parent. He told me every day for weeks how lucky I am.

It's just another pill. Speed, Demerol and marijuana were popular items at my house by the time I was fourteen. My father is quite 'cool'. He supplied the neighbor boys with booze, pot and a girl who had no understanding of boundaries. I had access to marijuana, Demerol, white cross (speed), black beauties and something called yellow microdot. I would discover these pharmaceuticals made life easier for me, though they only contributed to my memory lapses.

I don't know or question if everyone is as confused as I am about life. I was running away or kicked out of the house so often by the time I was sixteen, that I had a difficult time recalling how often I was living at home. I hated it there. I had a tree stump that I stayed in often. I ran away to it. I would lie about spending the night at a friend's house and go to my stump where I slept well. I lived in it on and off.

My mother is staying in Florida with her mother. I should know why she is there, but I don't. It's one of those blank spaces, lost time. While I find this aspect of my life bothersome, I accept this is the way things are for me.

I have moved into a small house with my dad's secretary, Lucille. Lucille is only five or six years older than me. We share a king-sized bed in a one bedroom house. I'm quite happy with the situation. I am still going to school. I still work at the café. I think I am free.

From a dead sleep, I roll over to see my father on top of Lucille. He is laughing at my confusion as I wake up realizing what they are doing.

I am completely disgusted.

Lucille at least had the grace to be aghast as I got my pillow and took a blanket and stormed out to the sofa in the other room.

She says something I can't make out, but I heard my father say clearly, "It isn't important, she won't care and she won't tell."

He was right, I never told anyone. However, I did care.

I didn't care that he was cheating on my mother. The cheating was old news for me. The first time I was aware of him with another woman was when I was in the first grade. I didn't tell then, either. I had been completely indoctrinated in my father's belief system from a very early age. What I thought or felt about anything didn't matter. What matters on this night is the same thing that always matters: what he wants, what he tells me to think and what he tells me to say.

I don't want to see these things or know about them. I want to be far away from my family. I drift back to sleep by the time he leaves. He feels the need to wake me up as he heads out the front door.

I realize by his parting comments that he thinks I left the bed because I was jealous!

The need to crawl out of my own skin is almost unbearable and sleep never returns on this night. That night cemented the fact that I cannot get away from him. No matter what I do, or where I go, he will always be there.

Restless to the point of distraction, I get up and read. Lucille finds me sitting on the sofa wrapped in a quilt still reading when she gets up for work this morning.

She asks, "Are you okay?"

"Sure!" I answer brightly. "I'm great. I slept so well – I woke up early is all."

What I really want to do is scream at her, call her bitch, whore and slut. I will never sleep in the bed again and I sleep on the sofa for the remainder of my stay there.

My father has a key and chuckles at me feigning sleep on the sofa as he passed through to the bedroom, or back out to his car. It's important to him that I be awake and aware of his presence.

I run to the tree regularly, wondering why I am paying rent.

False Hope

I MADE IT TO THE end; I'm out of here!

I am finally graduating from high school this year. My school counselor has been working to help me get into an art school and it looks good. I am going to study for two years in Florida and two years in Europe. The counselor persuaded them to overlook my math grades, which were abysmal, because my SAT scores were high enough. To be honest, none of my grades were that good. I cut school three days out of five. All through high school I had a tablet full of excuse notes. Dad signed all the sheets so I wouldn't bother him. If the school called, he verified the notes. He couldn't care less if I went to school. Mom? I guess we just avoided each other. I don't think she ever answered the phone. She must have been thrilled that it was almost over, too. They all talked about how wonderful life will be once I was gone for good.

I had GI bill benefits for college because of my father's disability. The school required the leftover $1,500.00 not covered to be paid up front. I knew this, and I'd been giving my father my paychecks for over a year. Six months before graduation I told him he needed to write the school a check.

He laughed at me. "A check? With what money?"

"What money?" I repeated, "The money I've been giving you for school for a year! You said you would keep it for me! You said to let you know when I needed it and you'd write the check because I'm not old enough to write a check!"

He sits there smugly smiling at me. I begin to feel disconnected and gray again. The reality is that he has been getting my paychecks for the last year and half my tips from working as a waitress. Sometimes he got all my tips. All the time he talked about how glad I would be to have that money for school when the time came.

My mother walks in and wants to know what is going on.

Dad says, "Oh, she thinks we have money for her to go to a fancy art school! As usual, she doesn't think about what anyone else needs."

I feel my heart thudding in my chest. I feel a little sick. No money! I can't save up that much money again. Going to school here ... oh God! I can't even think about it. All I can think about is being trapped here. Mom is looking at me with disgust. I know better than to argue about it. She will believe whatever he tells her.

There seems to be nothing left to say. I walk away and think about all the things that have gone on. Most of the time it makes my head spin, but today I reached some sort of impasse. That trapped, cornered feeling hasn't gone away. I've gone outside and I'm walking, more like marching up to the gravel pit above our house. It's quite a way off, but I need to walk off this frustration. I think about what my life has in store for me.

Stealing from the little corner store for him.

Watching him scratch his wounds with a wire brush from the garage.

Going from hospital to hospital for drugs.

Watching my mother sitting in the corner with her red lipstick and cigarettes, drinking wine all night, or at the table waiting for the spirits to come and write some message to her.

My father having the boys I go to school with over so he can offer my body to them.

Since the gun incident, he hasn't left any weapons out. I guess that got his attention. He still beats me. He still has all the control. He offers me more drugs and I take them.

I feel the grayness coming.

This time it feels good to surrender.

Freedom: The Marines

I'M TALKING TO MY BEST friend and tell her, "Come on. Let's go talk to the recruiters."

"What?" She is laughing, "You're crazy!"

"Let's just walk in and say, 'Hi, I want to sign up!'"

She says, "I'll go, but I'm not saying anything!"

We both laugh and we go into the building. My friend is afraid we will shoot our mouths off and be signed up. I'm not signing anything, this is just a lark. This is just something to do while we cut classes. As it turns out, they have things to talk about that interest me and I end up going back several times.

They really got my attention telling me boot camp was in South Carolina. I lived in California. I liked that I could go so far away. It's about as far as I can get. It had nothing to do with patriotism, the desire to learn a trade, or anything else. It is simple: I want out. I want to go as far away as I possibly can. I even asked the recruiter about going overseas.

"The Marine Corps?" My father is gleeful. "You want to join the Marines? Really?"

I'd just come home. The recruiter had called and spoken to him.

"Ha! Want to be just like your old man, eh?"

My parents are telling everyone how wonderful it is that I am so patriotic. They say that I am going into the Corps to be like my father because I look up to him. They say whatever makes them feel good.

Two years of duty and school is paid for. I wasn't sure I trusted them about the schooling. After all, I was supposed to be able to go to school on my dad's VA benefits because of his disability, but apparently, he can call the shots on that one. I've been through that already and I am still here. At least if I do get school benefits, now they are mine. Dad told everyone I was following his example; that I wanted to be like him.

I laugh at the thought.

All I have heard since he lost his legs is his damn pity-party bullshit. "I only have a few years to live," he says.

We are supposed to feel bad for him. All I pray for any more is for him to die a long, lingering, painful death. Live forever Daddy! Then die, alone and in a lot of PAIN! I am sick of all of this. He is going on about one of my girlfriends and what he would like to do to her. I can't have anyone over, since he'll sit around in his underwear, exposing himself. His friends are almost as bad. I need out!

So now, I don't have to worry about school or my family. I signed up in February right after my eighteenth birthday and I graduate in June. I will be gone in July. From here on out, it's parties and more parties.

Graduation lacks any of the excitement that normally accompanies this milestone. It is just something to get over with. There will be no party at my house.

No new dress or shoes because, as my mother said, "You will be wearing a graduation gown, who will see the new clothes? You don't need them."

We showed up, I walked, and we went home. I was disappointed to discover there was no actual diploma in the scroll they handed me. Someone told me to go pick it up.

As we drove home, I heard my father say loudly, "What a waste of time."

I went to other people's parties. There is a party at my house, but it wasn't for me, it was for my father. He tells me the boys are waiting their turn to try to get me into the bedroom. He is proud of this. I don't even realize I can say no.

There were a couple of boys I liked, but Dad, always in charge, wasn't having any of that. If he knew them well enough he would point out other girls that he thought were cuter and better. He would tell me I wasn't good enough for them. Who wants a slut and a whore?

July finally comes; I dress up to get on the plane. I feel full of myself and remarkably grown up. I've never really been away from home before. I think about my mother crying when my brother was learning to drive the tractor. She didn't cry when I was driving it. I had asked her why she was crying and she said, "Oh, your brother is driving and becoming a man."

Yeah, it was a real Kodak moment.

I'm getting on a plane, going to boot camp, and listening to how life is going to be better around the house when I am gone. No more fighting. No more dirty dishes in the sink. I am the oldest and apparently, I am a one-girl demolition team. I don't care. I don't have to live here anymore and that is all that matters to me.

I think about all the chores I do around the house and wonder who is going to do what I do. I keep my mouth shut. I'm not sure that they can't stop me from leaving. They had to give their permission for me to enlist, yet I still worry that until I am on that plane and it is in the air, somehow they could stop it.

I will miss Gabe the most. I hated leaving him alone with them, but I have to.

Out on the tarmac of this little airport, a shuttle plane is waiting, waiting for me! Just a few moments longer and I will have freedom. I can feel the blood rush through my veins in my excitement. No one has any great words of wisdom for me. There are no poetic goodbyes, just a sort of good riddance. It strikes me that my mother is standing there smiling. No tears of pride for the daughter that is growing up, I muse. I am too giddy with anticipation to lament the love she has never given me.

It's time to get on the plane. Right before I cross the tarmac, feeling the wind blowing in my face, the sun in my eyes; I turn towards them just in case they are doing something noteworthy, something to tell me they care at all. They aren't even waving. Gabe is. Bryan, the baby, is playing with a stick, probably killing bugs, he likes to do that. Mom and Dad are just there, looking the part. They are good at looking the part.

I will never talk about the past. I will make up new stories about a loving, happy family if the need arises.

I take that first step to the plane, walking, then running. I don't look back anymore.

Boot Camp

I AM GOING TO SAN Francisco to be processed. Then I'm off to Paris Island, South Carolina, for Boot Camp. I'm not even afraid. Looking back, I suspect my survival skills of being able to handle what was happening in the moment served me well. Moreover, when I got there they told us they would not hit us.

Hmm...

Dad told me they would beat on me better than he did. Once I knew they couldn't hit me, nothing else at Boot Camp was quite that bad.

Many of the people who knew my father when he was in the Marines were still around. I would run into them from time to time. Many of the stories they would tell about Dad were funny; however, there were other stories of my father losing rank for his shenanigans, disrespect and laziness.

The story he told everyone about the explosion that cost him his legs is a sham. I met one of the Marines who had been up in the tower when the explosions happened. I had wanted to believe my father's version of the story. I wanted to believe that he had done something altruistic for someone. These people had no reason to lie; they thought I knew the truth.

My father was a notorious liar. He left little, if anything for me to look up to, but at one point I had been proud to say he earned that medal. Now I have to wonder where he even acquired it.

I believed if he was good, then I was good. He was not good. So, what was I?

I keep running into people who knew him and who were not impressed. People who thought I might be a chip off the old block and a couple of men who thought I would sleep with them to get ahead.

"Aren't you Frenchie's kid?" they would ask in surprise when I deflected their advances.

Wearily, I would say, "Yes." Then I would smile and move on.

My first boss in the exchange system where I would be working made sure I was aware that he knew my father quite well and would not be putting up with 'any silly bullshit' while I was working for him.

"I run a clean shop," he told me brusquely.

I didn't defend myself, I simply said, "Yes, Sir. I understand, Sir!"

"I don't want to see my inventory shuffling out the door either!"

Again, I answer, "Yes, Sir."

"I will see you court marshaled if I need to."

Again, I don't defend myself, I just say, "Yes, Sir!"

If my father trained me well for anything, it was this. Do not say more than you have to and do not volunteer any information, thoughts or ideas. If you can possibly agree, do it and do it without explanations.

"Private, at ease!" He barks, "I want you to look at me!"

What I like about the Marines is that the rules never change. I can stand at attention, focus on the wall, answer the questions and be dismissed. Even "at ease" has a protocol. I can still "assume the position". I am a Marine. He barks and I don't even flinch. I show no emotion, no fear, nothing. I change my stance and look at the Gunny. He stares back, trying to read my face.

"I want no trouble from you. Are we clear?"

"Yes, Sir. Very clear, Sir."

In spite of my outward composure, I was wildly intimidated as he dismissed me. I was terrified of the man the whole time I was at his base. Lucky for me, I was in class most of the time. In the end, he had better things to do than check up on me all the time, or if he did, he found nothing. I never so much as picked up a paper clip that didn't belong to me.

Wedding Bells

I AM HAVING A GOOD time. I'm almost finished my classes and expect to be stationed in North Carolina. I'd go back to the barracks, the mess hall for dinner, then the NCO Club which was right next door for music, dancing, games and talking with lots of people. It's great fun.

One day, I'm at sick call with the flu, trying to figure out how to go to sleep in this miserable chair while I wait to see someone. I'm also mad because I had to walk over here so that someone would tell me I am too sick to go to work – but then I'll have to walk the mile back to the barracks to go back to bed. I'm sick and grumpy. I didn't even comb my hair this morning.

A man walks up and tells me, "You are the most beautiful girl I have ever seen."

I stare at him through bloodshot eyes, sniffle and croak out with my sore throat, "You must not get out much."

He smiles, "I heard you were funny."

I'm not feeling very funny. I don't know who he is, and tell him so. He assures me he has seen me over at the club and has been working up the nerve to talk to me. I smile in spite of myself. He is cute and the flattery doesn't hurt. He is standing there rocking on his feet a little. He is a little older than I am and as sure of himself as only a young Marine can be.

"The Marine Corps Ball is coming up soon. Would you go with me?"

I was thunderstruck! I really wanted to go to the ball, but had no date. I hadn't gone to my junior or senior proms in high school.

"We can sit with your friends if you like," he assures me. We would laugh about it later when he admitted he thought I'd say no.

I barely saw him before the big night. I had duty in the barracks, work, drill and classes. I had to find something to wear at what was now the last minute, and I had no car. He turned out to be the perfect date. Pulling out chairs, opening doors, and fetching me whatever he thought I might need. He was clearly proud that I was with him and I thought he was just beautiful in those dress blues.

We were inseparable after that. We saw each other as much as our schedule would allow. We took a couple of road trips. I met his parents and they appeared to like me. I liked them.

We had so much fun.

I called home to tell my parents I was getting married.

While I don't recall all the details of the conversation, I remember my father's bone chilling threat.

"If you do this, I will tell him everything you have done, and he won't want you. You're a slut. I will tell him about you and me."

I was terrified of the consequences; however, in an uncharacteristic moment of defiance, I dared him to tell. "Go ahead and tell. You can't tell anyone!"

I got off the phone and got myself married shortly after. It was so easy. We ran off to the courthouse and were married by a judge with two of our friends standing up for us. He wasn't mean to me and I thought it must be love. There was some drug use and rumors about his father sending a blank check to a judge to get him out of trouble. However, we didn't talk about it. I didn't think it was odd not to talk about it either. Why would I?

At first, we didn't have enough money to get a place together. So, we lived in the barracks for another month before moving into a little place just outside of the base. One of the bedrooms was just big enough for a twin bed and the master bedroom was big enough for a double if you didn't want to walk around too much. I don't even know where our furniture came from. I was accustomed to things with my parents just showing up or disappearing. I never asked where it all came from and the information was never volunteered. The place was filthy. We cleaned it up, spending half our paychecks on food and cleaning supplies.

I was happy because I no longer had my father's last name. I did miss the barracks and my friends, and I just sort of lurched along doing whatever I thought I should be doing.

For me, this marriage was a divorce from my father. I was happy. Dad was furious. I would soon discover he had very long arms.

The first person to contact me was Eddie. He was an enlisted man who lived down the street from us in the trailer park when I was a kid. He is a captain now. I was invited to dinner and was incredibly self-conscious. Being fresh out of Boot Camp made me acutely aware of our differences: I was enlisted and he was an officer. He picked me up at the barracks and drove me to his place over in base housing. I found myself answering his questions with 'yes, Sir' and 'no, Sir'. He assured me that it wasn't necessary to refer to him that way in his home. However I couldn't help it.

While he was talking, I thought that since he was my father's friend, this couldn't be good. He was not my friend. Daddy's friends were not good people nor were they generally smart people. They were people who did his bidding without asking too many questions. In my eyes, these people were just extensions of him, doing the same things.

I ate dinner and listened to stories about the old days. I answered questions about how my training was going. I tell him it is going well, I like it. I was to work in the Post Exchange (PX) in management but first had to work my way through from the warehouse up. I was getting comfortable. His wife is nice and much as I remember her to be when I was eleven years old. They have a boy and a girl who are younger than I am and though I remember them, I never really played with them. I don't think the kids remembered me at all.

Eddie has finally gotten to the real reason for this visit and dinner. He has asked me come into the other room now that dinner is over. His wife declines my offer to help with the dishes, telling me that her husband has many questions about my father's health and how his life is turning out.

We spend a few minutes talking about just that. There isn't much to tell about my father's life that he doesn't already know. I'm not sure what is fine to tell. Dad doesn't like his life talked about and I am sure that this is not what Eddie wants to discuss anyway. I don't have to wait too long. He stands up and looks a little uncomfortable pacing around the room a bit. He is tall and a bit imposing.

He takes a deep breath and starts to tell me everything that is wrong with my marriage, my situation and my new husband. I'm too young. I'm naïve. My husband is older and a troublemaker. My husband is only three years older! The Captain wants to talk about my career. Really, I've just begun my life and have no precedent for this type of conversation.

My parents never talked to me about how to live my life. No one talked to me about morals. The only conversation we had about marriage was that I was cute and could expect to marry a doctor or lawyer. This meant I would be taken care of for the rest of my life. No education needed. My parents didn't think I was going to amount to much of anything on my own.

Dad's advice was to use my body to get whatever I wanted or needed.

I am being told that my father called to discuss my future and all the folks back home are worried about me. Now Eddie tells me he is concerned as well. I'm too young to be married. I should be working on improving myself. Improving myself? I don't know what this means. He says my new husband is a drug peddler! What? My confusion is palpable. To make things worse, I have to admit I am married to someone I barely know.

What if all this was true?

I didn't know what to make of this information nor did I know how to reply. This was a new game I've never played. Dad never had anyone else do his dirty work. Besides that, why did he care I was or wasn't married? I didn't understand. Much of what was said to me was foreign. I couldn't even comprehend the fact that we were having a conversation like this. Not that I wasn't intelligent enough; I just had no base to work from. Dad, who always called me a whore and a slut, was worried about who married me? I didn't think I could feel confused by my family from so far away, but I was.

It's a long and quiet drive back. Though I think about all that has been said to me on the drive home, I get out of the car, walk through the door, and I forget the whole thing. It's not important. They are three thousand miles away. They can't tell me what to do. These people don't know what they are talking about.

What a crock! I tell myself this the next day, but I begin to worry. Just what is my father telling people? He knows people here. He wrote letters to my drill instructor in Boot Camp and caused problems for me. I've already been lectured at length about causing problems when I have done nothing.

There had been a couple of drug parties at my new house. I don't really care about it. I grew up around so many drugs and alcohol I didn't think it was a big deal. I'm not doing anything, so I think I can't get into trouble. I am hearing from my father through various venues that my new husband has had quite a few problems in the past with the law. The rumor is told to me again that his father sent a blank check to a judge to get him out of trouble. My husband denies this vehemently.

I don't really know what to think or believe any more. I don't care enough, or love this guy enough to continue with the barrage of negative bullshit coming at me. Sadly, I don't believe that I am even loved. I believe what I have been told; I'm just the prize. No one can really love me. It never occurred to me that I could hurt someone because they love me. I was having a good time. Now I wasn't. I wanted out. Dad kept calling me, almost daily. I am reminded how relentless my father can be.

He told me he retained a lawyer for me. It won't cost me anything and I won't have to come home. I'm getting divorced, and I don't have any control over it. I don't know how to extricate myself from my father's grip even as a young adult so many miles away.

I've been offered orders to go to Virginia and I accept. I'm told I don't have to take them, as there are openings in my Military Occupation Skill here.

"No," I say to my Sergeant, "I'll take them."

I don't say I need to get out of here. I can't even articulate why I need or want to leave.

The divorce has a life of its own. No one asks me anything. The lawyer talks to my father. I let him be served with the divorce papers without saying a word. He confronts me and I finally tell him something that makes no sense to either of us. I just babbled about having a career, getting orders, whatever came to mind in that panicked moment. I will not say that my father is relentlessly calling. I will not say that my father has secrets to tell about me. I can only get myself out of a situation that has become unmanageable for me. I am isolated with my secrets.

I tell him the marriage is over. He thinks there is someone else. There is not. It might be better for him to think that than to hear any stories from my father.

I pack what little I have and never look back.

New Beginnings

I LIKE MY NEW BASE and my new job. I'm so proud to be a Marine that I get accused of having green blood. I always laugh and say, "As long as it's Marine Green!"

I work a lot at the stores, but I think it's fun. I enjoy the people I work with. No one sat me down to tell me not to act like my father with their stories of his pranks and thievery.

My first Sergeant at the barracks has me come to her office. She tells me I can't date until the divorce is over. I wonder how she even knows about it. When I finally ask, she smiles and tells me she got a letter from my father.

"He is quite concerned about you," she says. "And, we do have rules about these things. I will let you know when you can resume dating. It will protect you and your reputation as well as the reputation of the Corps."

"Yes, Ma'am."

As I prepare to leave, she says softly, "I used to know your father. I was sorry to hear what happened to him."

I don't know what to say to her. So again, I say, "Yes, Ma'am." It seems like a safe reply. My heart is pounding and it hurts. I feel a little light-headed. She is looking at me, waiting for something. I can't think of anything intelligent to say. I am wondering if she can see that I feel sick and am starting to sweat a little. I'm sure they will be talking or writing again and I fear what Dad will say. I fear what has already been said. What does she know? Neither of us is saying anything and it is uncomfortable. I am desperately trying to think of something to say when she finally tells me I can go.

I don't talk with her again until the divorce was final for a couple of weeks. She tells me I can go on dates now.

I say, "Yes, Ma'am, I know."

She gives me a strange look and lets me go. I had received the divorce papers in the mail. I assumed my father would be letting her know all the important details of my life and this look from her was proof.

I believe no one can be trusted. Daddy knows a lot of people. If he doesn't know them, he pulls the war hero racket he has going and calls them anyway. I don't know who he talks to, but to me, everyone is now a suspect.

He is in my head all the time. He told me to call home once a week. I make $125 every two weeks and a $25 bond comes out of that, so I call collect. He answers the phone most of the time, happy to take the call. I don't even know what we talk about. I'm trying to live my life, trying to keep him happy and quiet. I discover quickly that it's easier to navigate the world without his name. I have dragged my feet in getting my name changed since the divorce. No one knows who my father is since I came to this base.

Daddy keeps raising the point, "Why don't you change your name back?"

I tell him, "I will. I'm just busy."

We have this talk week after week. It takes me a year to take back my maiden name. I'm in no hurry to be visibly attached to him. By the time I change it, no one I work with cares. I have been around long enough to prove myself.

I'm no longer connected to my father.

Home for Christmas

LIFE IS GOOD FOR A while and I decide to go home for Christmas. I haven't been home since I left for boot-camp over a year ago and have convinced myself it will be okay. I will go home like everyone else this year.

My friends are going home for holidays and I want to be like them. I'm acutely aware I am not like them. I want to go home and come back with stories about family, love and friends. So what if they used to hit me. Lots of people hit their kids.

Little by little, I have unconsciously begun rewriting my history, and day by day I start believing it.

I'm a new person. They like me at work. I don't lose time anymore. I'm not confused about what I have done or where I have been. I don't get blamed for things I can't call to mind. I am strong. I have thrived in the order and discipline around me. I am a Marine. No one can hurt me.

I fill in the holes of my memory with other people's stories. I weave them into my own family and I begin to believe the stories are mine. It's so easy.

The house is filthy. I have to clean the bathroom before I want to use it. The toilet is vivid proof that three boys live there and there is a ring around the bathtub you could scrape with a knife. It amuses my mother when I ask for cleaning supplies. I spent two hours cleaning the bathroom so I could use it, trying to remember if it was that dirty when I lived there. I don't think it was.

There is general disarray about the house that surprises me. They have acquired a bird. Its cage is perched at the end of the counter between the kitchen and the dining room. It's dirty. There are seeds everywhere, the counter, the floor and sprinkled in amongst the papers and pile of old mail sitting next to it. I am shocked that this mess is so close to where my father cooks.

The first day is okay. I visit some friends around town and have a fairly good time. I see an old crush and wonder briefly 'what if.' The thought passes quickly.

What if? I ask myself. The answer is I would be here. I'd never leave and life would never have changed. I would be nobody; a nobody having babies. Where would I work – the cafe?

I go to another party and kids I used to know are there, some with babies already. There is plenty of beer and pot. I look to the corner where a baby is crying and see the mother blowing smoke from her joint into the kid's face. Eventually the crying stops. I understand I don't belong here anymore and I leave the party.

My parents are up when I get home and surprised to see me come in so early. "Didn't you have fun?" my mother asks.

"It was okay."

I tell them about the baby. What had happened really bothered me. I knew it was wrong. They both look at me blankly. They don't see anything wrong with it. I start crying and I don't know why. They continue to stare at me, then each other saying nothing. I tell them I'm going to bed.

Bed. Sleep. A whole new issue. I shouldn't have come here. I think it's too quiet, which is a first for this house. I must be used to the barracks and the constant rustle of the other girls I live with.

That doesn't make any sense. I can hear the TV in the other room. I can hear the rustling of my brothers in the room next door. Really, it isn't quiet at all. Don't they know it's late? People are trying to sleep! I'm swinging back and forth on a pendulum of emotions.

I get up and look out the sliding glass door of my room. It is total blackness outside. A few pinpoint lights way across the field. No moonlight tonight. I check the lock on the sliding glass door. It's locked tight. There is a broomstick stuck in the other side along the track and I make sure it won't slip. Yep. Not going anywhere. I get back into the bed. I still toss and turn. My heart is hammering and I am getting a headache. I can't get up and go out to the front room. I get an adrenaline rush and wonder if I could be having a heart attack. What's the matter with me? I don't know why I feel this way, but God knows I am not going out to the other room. I am not asking for any aspirin.

I get up and push my bed up against the door and I'm asleep before my head hits the pillow.

I'm awake just as the sun is coming up in the morning. It is pretty outside. I've always thought this was beautiful country. It takes a minute for me to wonder why I can look out the glass door like that. Now, in the daylight, I feel fine. What was wrong with me? I set it aside and reproach myself for being so juvenile and hope no one knows how ridiculous I have been. I quietly push the bed back where it belongs and slip out to go for a run.

It doesn't feel like winter to me. It was quite cold back east when I got on the plane. The sun is out and it feels good on my skin. As I run, I start to wonder how I am going to make it through two weeks. I run faster and faster until I am sprinting. I won't make it! I won't make it! My brain is screaming with the pounding of my feet: left, right, left, right. I'm weak. I head back for the house.

I can smell the bacon cooking before I come into the house. Dad must be up. I go up the drive and take a deep breath before I go inside. He is startled to see me standing there.

"I thought you were still asleep!"

"Went for a run," I answer.

"I used to run, I liked it too."

"Really? I don't remember that about you." I think about it for a minute.

"Oh well, you wouldn't remember, I did it at the base," was his swift reply.

I let it go. I have been in the Corps long enough to know where he worked. Running was a requirement, as was marching. That's my Dad, consummate storyteller, legendary liar and con man. I wanted to stop this before I got sucked into some other story.

"Do you need help, or can I go take a shower before breakfast is ready?"

"Hand me that pot, then go," he says.

I remember the water problems, so I try to hurry. As the water just begins to get warm I hear a pot slam into the wall and cursing to go with it.

"Wonderful," I say to myself. "Nothing has changed."

My hand is shaking so badly that I keep dropping the bar of soap.

"Just get rinsed and get out," I tell myself. Though the water is hot, I am shivering as I rinse off the soap. I make a note to talk to the doctor at sick call about this tremor in my hand. It's getting worse. He said it was hereditary last time I mentioned it, but it is becoming bothersome.

I take my time getting dressed, hoping he will be over his tantrum before I emerge. Whatever has set him off couldn't possibly have anything to do with me, could it? Nevertheless, I drag myself off the bed and into the hallway with trepidation.

He seems to be over it. He tells me to set the table and I'm glad to have something to do. Everyone is up and moving around now. My brothers are looking forward to a big breakfast. They eat like lumberjacks and are built like them, too. John is having six eggs! I weigh in at 110 pounds and I'm 5'1". My dad used to call me the runt of the litter. Breakfast is amazing. Dad has put on quite a show of a meal. I have a piece of toast and a couple pieces of bacon with orange juice.

"What about the home fries and eggs?"

"Oh God, Dad! I can't eat all this!" I exclaim as he piles up my plate.

I have a memory coming that I want to forget about. I remember him filling my plate and making me eat until I was ill. Would he do that now? No way! I'm not sure.

Breakfast is completed with little grumbling. The dog is stealing food from Dad's plate and he has thrown a thing or two over his shoulder for the dog to catch. It's always a show with him, but at least it's quiet. Daddy is bothered that I don't eat enough and makes a couple of comments before he lets it go. After breakfast he goes down to his shop. No one knows what he is doing down there. No one follows him to see if he needs help. Everyone seems to sigh at the reprieve. My brothers and I joke a bit while doing the dishes. I tease my baby brother who has grown a foot since I left. They seem to be okay. I don't ask. It isn't the way we do things. Each person in the family is on their own isolated island. No information passed or offered either way. We smile. We tell everyone everything is great.

Before I lose my nerve, I go find my mother. I tell her, "I am leaving the day after tomorrow."

She looks stunned, "Why?"

"Why?" It's my turn to look surprised. "The yelling and screaming and the pots being thrown around this morning are a good start. I can't take it, I am shaking so bad I had trouble holding a cup of coffee this morning. I have to leave and I have already changed the reservation. I'm sorry, I just can't be here."

I offer all this in a rush. She wants to discuss it and I have nothing else to say.

"Did you tell your father?"

"Not yet," I sigh in defeat. "I changed the ticket and I can't change it back again."

She is cow-eyed. She can't be expecting me to believe she cares if I stay.

She doesn't. She finally asks, "Will you tell him why you are leaving?"

"No, Mother, I won't. I will think of something else." I say quietly.

She is relieved.

I arrive back at the base a couple of days later. When my friends come back from their vacations, they ask about my trip. I regale them with the antics of my baby brother, good food, gifts I had taken and how everyone loved them. That part was true. I spent a lot of money on gifts that year. I even talked about Christmas dinner and what a wonderful cook my father was.

"I had a wonderful, marvelous time." I said. "I can't wait to do it next year!"

I didn't know why I was lying about it all, I didn't ponder it. I let it go. Somehow, it didn't feel like a lie. Everyone has these amazing family stories. They keep asking for mine.

Do they want to hear my real family stories?

Probably not.

Does continuing to lie about my real family make me a bad person?

Probably.

Annie's Silent Partner

MY FATHER TERRORIZED AND ABUSED other children in the neighborhood. The story that follows belongs to one of them. She held the missing pieces of my life and when she gave her story to me, it literally brought me to my knees for two days while I absorbed it all. Somehow I believed it couldn't have happened to anyone else. I was careful to never let my friends be alone with him. Their families were so much better than mine. Appearances are deceiving.

I was shared violently.

She was shared violently.

She was battered by her mother and my father used that information to keep her under control. She had no reason to trust her mother would help her.

This went on under the noses of the very people who should have been protecting their own children. Shame on them, shame on everyone who has a child and is so self-absorbed and selfish they would rather look the other way than do the right thing and stop it.

She has asked to be identified only as "Annie's Silent Friend." This story is in support of mine. Most importantly this is *her* story. It deserves to be told, heard and read. I am proud of her. I want her to know I love her.

I DO NOT REMEMBER THE exact age Annie and I became close friends. I know we were very young, in grade school she was a very close friend for many years.

I always felt she was treated very badly by her parents, especially her father. My own mother was very abusive, physically and emotionally. We never talked about it at the time. Secrets run deep.

Her mother made very beautiful dolls. One day, after Annie had joined the Marines and left, I asked her to make one for my mother. The clothing was made from the same fabric used for the curtains in my grandmother's room. The hair was made from my mother's hair. The doll was beautiful and in the course of making the doll we became close. I also developed a relationship with Annie's brother.

John was good-looking young guy with a great sense of humor. In the beginning, when his arms were around me I felt safe. I spent a lot of time at Annie's parents' house with him and before long we became sexually active. I adored him.

His father, Bryan, (who will forever after be called That Bastard Bryan), was doing artwork made of copper sheets for a man who owned a motel. He was very artistic and was always doing something creative. I was fascinated. He had a small shop, separate from the main house, where he worked on these projects. In his shop and the home Annie grew up in, he began to molest me and would continue to do so for many years. I saw no way out.

I was so very young. He would tell me I looked like Mona Lisa. They held séances and practiced ghost writing sessions that took place at their large harvest style dining table. We played dominoes, too. He found many instances where he could fondle me and make angry statements about his wife.

The fondling eventually progressed to full blown intercourse. I was terrified to say anything. I had feelings for his son. My father was a police officer. My mother was beating me. When it all started, I did not understand what was going on. Nothing like this had ever happened to me before. In the beginning, I mistook a little attention for true caring. A time finally came when I stopped having anything at all to do with the whole family. I stopped going the house. I stopped seeing Annie's brother. I thought it was over. I thought it was as simple as just staying away from there.

That Bastard Bryan showed up at my house showing his copper pictures to my mother, who I was in great fear of. I sat there listening as he patiently explained to her that he was teaching art classes. He told my mother what a great job I had done helping him with this particular piece. He told her I had talent and he only wanted me to continue with his classes. What a shame it would be if I didn't continue with the lessons. My mother proudly agreed with him.

So, I started going back to the "classes" and to what would become a little shop of horrors.

When I would not show up, John would come pick me up. But, there was no date with the good looking son I had adored. One time, they took me back to That Bastard's house. John left and I was left lying on the floor hog-tied with sticks poked down my pants. Gabe was then forced to untie me and leave. His father was brutally mean to him and told him to get out with dire threats. We were all afraid of him. More than once I witnessed Gabe beaten to the ground both inside and outside the house. They would threaten the horrible things they would do if he did not run and hide or if he told his mother anything. I was raped by him or sometimes by both him and his war veteran/hero buddy Fang together. When it was over, I was allowed to leave. I walked home through several acres of hayfields and would stop and bathe in the creek on the way.

I later learned I was not the only victim in our little community. There were many others. One of those was a young girl brought home by his son, just as I was. She became pregnant by him. Not by the son, but by That Bastard. He had his son do the dirty work and take her for an abortion. Four other young females who lived not far from his home were also victims.

The abuse continued to escalate as I grew older. I had always wondered if he had done all this to Annie as well. My gut told me he had, even though I did not know for sure. There was also abuse in his son's mobile home that sat next to the shop of horrors. When his son was away he and Fang would use it instead of the shop. He also provided drugs and alcohol to many of his victims.

When I got older, I met someone, fell in love and got married. When that That Bastard Bryan discovered it, he convinced the man I married to join the Marine Corps. That Bastard is a slick talker and he got rid of the competition or the threat and he continued to try molesting me. I left the area.

That Bastard Bryan told one of my friends that he was going to divorce his wife to be with her. When she got pregnant, he wanted nothing more to do with her. She was just a kid. We all were. None of us told; they were war heroes. Who would believe a bunch of small town kids?

Somehow his wife found out about the pregnancy. I vividly remember the day Annie's mother arrived at my home. She spoke with my mother about the young gal who had become pregnant. She told my mother that she was planning to leave her husband.

Annie's mother and mine asked if he had ever done anything to me. Out of fear, I lied. I told them both no, and did not say anything about the other girls I had learned about. I didn't tell about her son. I didn't tell about the other boys in the Old Bastard Bryan Club. I didn't tell about the woman, the nurse who had been coming to their home.

The nurse was from a local hospital and I remember he made her walk around the house with a dildo inserted in her. He would comment and laugh about it. She didn't seem to mind. He had previously shown this same sexual device to me several times calling it Mr. Squiggly. He loved to show us how it could shoot out liquid.

When he was finally divorced by his wife, he married the nurse. He moved into to her home and raised Annie's baby brother, Bryan. His stupid wife moved to another state and left her baby boy with That Bastard! Many years later I saw Gabe at a family wedding. He was so full of hate towards his father. He let me know his marriage had ended because of something their father had done to his new family. He did not go into any details. He and I both knew the details did not need to be discussed. Shortly after, everyone lost contact with him and have not heard from him since; strange, since my brother and him had been the best of friends. He has cut himself away from his entire family and all of his childhood friends.

I have carried the scars of this abuse my whole life. I've had a lot of counseling. The results were good. Counseling is hard work. I later became a foster parent to try to help children who were in the state system for the same types of abuse Annie and I have suffered. They ranged in age from six months old to seventeen years old. Yes, believe it. Infants that young are molested and are raped. I finally reconnected with Annie after many years. I never knew where she went. Her parents would only tell me she was gone. She could have been dead. I missed her. It opened up wounds I thought were gone. I came to realize the scars are never gone. Mine had been buried in a very deep, dark place within myself.

When I learned she had written one book and was working on the second, I knew I needed to read it. We talked about her book and what it was about. She believed I didn't know. Before I read it, I opened up to her about my own experiences. I wanted to let her know she was not alone in this nightmare of a life all those years ago. I wanted her to know I knew her story would be true. We cried and talked more. Annie will always remain very special to me and a very close friend. I feel like her silent partner. Annie will never know how very proud of her I am for doing what she has done with her life. Against all the odds she has so many accomplishments to be proud of.

My biggest regret is not admitting the day I was questioned by Annie's mother and mine, that yes, I was a victim. I still hate him today. I think I am angered most by the fact that her mother refuses to read her book or even acknowledge the fact that it is all true and did happen! When Annie and I talked she told me that she told her mother a long time ago, when she was still in counseling, that she was writing a book. Her mother said, according to Annie, and I do believe her, "I'm sure it will do very well. I will never read it."

I personally feel that all along she did know. I believe she turned a blind eye to the whole situation. It took place for many, many years and if I am ever able to obtain an address I will tell this woman so! The molestation took place in the home, the little shop of horrors, and in the brother's trailer. Her golden son, whom I had dated, was only picking me up and leaving me alone with his father. When I heard That Bastard had died, I was a happy person because I knew he'd never do this to anyone else again.

When I read Annie's book, a lot came flooding back. Before I turned the first page I knew what was going to come. I am Annie's silent partner. I know there are many others who will probably never come forward and support Annie in her truths about his crimes. I am sure there are things that are still blocked from my memories as they are from hers. Annie says our minds protect us. Maybe she is right.

Annie, I love you! I am proud of you! I feel the book you are writing should be read by every Department of Child and Family Services case workers and victims' advocates. They can learn from it and understand, really understand, the underlying factors why children run away from home, become rebellious, get into drugs and don't tell. These children are angry and commit suicide at very young ages, as teenagers and young adults. They have no one to trust. It isn't as simple as saying you will help them.

Annie, had it not been for your bravery, writing your book, I would not be here now telling my story. I must admit I did have a lot of nightmares. My emotions have been going everywhere again after reading book one and two last year. I have had to put all of this back into perspective where it belonged before I could sit down and write this for the final book.

You have my permission to use this information in your trilogy as long as I am referred to as a silent partner.

I love you. Hugs always,

Your Silent Partner

Journal Entries

IN MARCH 1988, WHEN I was in my early thirties, I completely fell apart. I stayed in the hospital for two months, unable to function. I then spent two years on disability, unable to function. After that, I went on to almost ten years of both group and private therapy. These entries are a reflection of the time when my life was at its darkest.

February 1988 (One week before admission to the hospital)

That stupid son-of-a-bitch-bastard-ass-hole. Why does my father get to go about his life? Why, after all this time, am I thinking about this garbage? Life is hard enough! Why am I thinking like this? It can't be real? I feel so bombarded! Fragments, pictures, incomplete thoughts flash into my head. I hit myself to get it out of my head but they don't leave. Waves of feeling him touch me. I take scalding hot showers to try to get clean. I am never clean. His blood is in my veins. I want it out. My skin is crawling and I can't get away.

I am sick.

I am losing it.

Why did he do that?

Why!!!

When he dies I want to see maggots eat his eyes out. I will shove a red hot poker into his eyes. I hate him.

March 1988 (First entry while in the hospital)

I am losing my mind!

I can't concentrate on anything.

I drive down the freeway and think how easy it would be to just turn and drive off the bridge.

I'm losing control.

I have been locking myself in rooms, don't answer the phone, and have to take huge amounts of Sominex to sleep.

I just want to be alone and when I am I'm terrified.

I want to die and can find no way to do it. I'm afraid I will not die and only make it worse.

I am not only ruining my life, but also the lives of my children.

I've finally become such an utter failure in my personal life that it is rubbing off into my professional life.

I have become a failure!

A failure with crazy thoughts and memories.

My skin crawls with the thought.

Isn't any of this enough? My God! Where is God for me?! Where has HE been while all this is going on? Where has HE been my whole fucking life!

I can't keep him away! No one can.

HE WILL COME. YOU DON'T KNOW HIM!

I WAS SPAWNED BY THE DEVIL. HOW CAN ANYONE UNDERSTAND ME?

March 1988

Ramona keeps promising that no one will see this. I only need to show it to her if I want to and if I bring it to talk about. She will not ask to touch it or look at it. It is mine. Fair enough if it's true. You can bet if anyone reads this I am never going to get out of here.

I have to be tough, I have to take it. I have to. If no one knows my pain and how much I loved them then they won't be able to laugh at me for being so stupid. It's tattooed on my forehead. See how much she can take. See how much she can screw things up. I'm so covered with scabs and scars that no one can get in and I can't get out. I'm in my own prison right inside my own head. I'm so lonely. I'm not feeling so tough and in control right now.

I had everything to lose. I lost it. I started over and I lost it again. Maybe I was kidding myself. Maybe I was supposed to die and this is all a big mistake. Maybe that bastard was supposed to kill me and fucked it up! I'm not supposed to be here. I feel like I am reliving someone else's nightmare. I am afraid. I'm afraid of whom I might, or might not be, afraid of what someone has seen. I'm afraid of what I may have done! I must look nuts with all this going on non-stop in my head. THIS CAN'T BE ME. What has happened for me to end up here?

I can't be good enough. I never deserve honesty or effort. I'm too dirty, too annoying, too this, too that, till everyone is gone. All of them... gone. Always they are gone and I am alone with this crazy shit in my head that I can't shut off anymore! I try till I disappear into the trying!

I don't know how to make my husbands love me back. One beat me. Another drinks too much. They cheat, lie, and make it clear I am not enough!

I didn't get the person I married. I wish you were my sister. I don't know who you are. They find out and they leave for sure!

I tried, please, please. Please help me. Please don't tell me no. When I'm told no I don't think I can stand it anymore. There have been so many no's in my life. Big NO and little no. All N-O's lead to me. OH MY FUCKING GOD HELP ME! I have become crazy as bat shit! They don't know who I am! I DON'T KNOW WHO I AM!

Maybe I am a killer. Maybe I am a whore! Maybe I am selfish, stupid, self-centered and only care about myself! Maybe I brought all this on myself! Maybe it really is my own fault.

I want to tell someone what happened. I want to tell but I can't. My throat closes and my tongue won't work. I don't think anyone understands that the words just will not come out. It's so ugly. I will shrivel into dust if the words come out. I try, they won't. Not even just one word. I know if I tell something awful, something unspeakable will happen. I have to keep sitting in that room. I HATE HIM! I HATE MY LIFE! He will come after me for telling, then what? It's easy to say to me that I need to talk about it. What will you do when he shows up? What then!

I know what it's like to be not worth the effort, the bother. Do you? Life is going on all around me and I don't know how to play the game. I'm on the outside looking in. I feel I shouldn't be here, that my life is only a shadow. I'm out of place, out of step. I'm always wrong. I so desperately want to be right, good, deserving and loved.

Why do I have to remember? I don't want to remember anything! I remember! I don't want to remember! I remember and I wish I had just driven off the bridge to make it stop.

May 1988 (After going home)

Ramona says write affirmations. Post them around the house. Look at them, read them and believe them. Uh sure. So I write them every day like a bad little kid writing on the blackboard after school. The girls asked me what the heck I was doing and want to be the ones to tape them around the house. They think it's fun. Who knew? My children love my therapy. I wish I was loving it. It feels hard. I don't want to do it anymore, but I am in too far to quit now.

Ramona says for every negative you hear it takes at least ten positives to make it go away. I probably won't live long enough but here goes.

May 1988

I've been trying to sort out the last few days and what is going on with me. I'm lots better about some things and not so much better about others. I don't have the wild memories so much anymore, when I do I hate it. Right now to know me is to know pain, confusion, loneliness, grief and change. I'm up, I'm down, I'm happy, I'm sad, and angry all at once. More in charge, less in charge, still afraid and untrusting.

May 1988

I'm supposed to write a list of what I want out of a relationship.
I have to write things I'll never get.
I'm willing to settle for much less.

I'm afraid of losing what little I have if I actually write it all down.
I have to write it down.
I have to make an honest list.
I have to be honest and write it down.
Please God, help me. I'm so afraid.
Maybe all I have to do is look at this differently.
Head toward your goal, even if it seems a long way off.
Nothing and no one will carry you, you will have to carry yourself.
By trying to maintain absolute control, you have none.

Once you accept that you are the cause of your struggle you can then affirm with certainty that it can be eliminated.

May 1988

Ramona says I need to keep working on my affirmations. She likes them. I hate them.

I sat in Ramona's office and squirmed, then cried because I couldn't think of one and she had to finally help me. Maybe someday I won't need the list, maybe someday I'll just know.

June 1988

Everyone has gone on with their lives without me. Everyone I went to high school with, everyone I was a kid with grew up and knew what to do. I got left behind and I've been running to catch up ever since. I just run and run and run. I don't know where to go or how to get there.

I think that somewhere inside I have finally decided I am not ever going to catch up. I just started in a different place. Do you know what I mean? My life? It feels like, well, like I give up. I'll just do it this way, Like other people are telling me. Counselors. It can't get any worse. I guess I know how I feel more than I know the words to describe it.

It's like this. If ten people were running a race and each has their own individual timer, I was the tenth person to leave yet I was trying to catch up with the first one that left. I couldn't catch them and now I realize I never will. It's not great, it's just OK. It has to be OK because there isn't anything else. I can't change it. I would like to be able to say it's great, but I can't. I just can't. It isn't great at all. I hate it! This is what I hate. I DON'T KNOW HOW TO MOVE FORWARD! I FEEL FROZEN!

I know I'm not going to die, it just feels like I'm going to be alone and I am afraid of being alone. I haven't shriveled up and gone crazy, yet. I've been finding things to do and keep busy. It's finally dawning on me that I can't make anyone love me. No matter what I do, I can't make anyone do or feel anything. I don't have that kind of power.

I told Ramona it was a relief, she said maybe it's more an acceptance that I need to accept things that I can't change, letting go of that kind of energy. Maybe she's right.

August 1988

Acceptance.

In the beginning, somewhere in my past I thought I had that kind of power. I wasn't good enough. Why can't you be like that kid? They would scream the question at me. I guess I have always thought I should have that kind of power. I just had to be...whatever it was, some magical sort of being I guess. I could make my husband, Dad, Mom, everyone, or anyone, love me. I found the formula. If I did everything just right, if I did everything I was supposed to be doing I could make them all love me.

Then when I got married I had to really make sure I got it all right. It's exhausting to keep it up. Even when I believed it was possible it was hard as hell. Sounds stupid eh? Well it's what I thought and it's how I have lived my life. I thought everyone else just knew how. I had to do everything right, more than right, more than perfect. I constantly worry about not being good enough. It's a relief to be alone and not have to worry about it.

One husband drank every day. He told me that it was my fault that he had to drink because I didn't have dinner ready for him when he got home. He got home two hours before me! I took on that responsibility by getting a crock pot!

I've lived my life knowing I must take care of myself and never, ever be a burden to anyone. You can get real wrapped up in that. It's complicated to try to explain.

Ramona asked me if I create situations? Well, maybe. I don't know. I pour all this energy into my relationships and they don't work. I pick people who are not healthy for me, then I work at it till I can't stand it anymore. Do I really do that? I have to admit that I begin to feel trapped. I felt a little trapped in this conversation but she doesn't let me off the hook.

Being needed. She says it isn't a particularly healthy type of relationship, for the relationship, or for me. I told her I don't know how to think about that.

It's hard work, it's uncomfortable as Ramona said in session today, "It's like having an empty bucket with a hole in it."

You keep doing this, shoveling it in, and it's never enough. It's always empty and NOTHING, NOTHING is ever enough. I'm not sure that feeling is really gone though. It's gone today and it wasn't there yesterday, but . . . I don't think it just magically went away.

Ramona says it might not ever completely go away for me. Maybe I should just try to be more comfortable, not perfect. I don't like this much, I have to keep telling myself to be happy with what I've got. It would be anyone I would be involved with. What kind of life is that for me? She has really given me a lot to think about. And I don't want to think about it.

September 1988

The first time I gave myself permission to acknowledge what I want and who I am, I wrote it and then I read it onto a cassette. I read it out loud, alone, and only once. I'm was terrified.

WHO AM I? NO ONE THAT ANYBODY KNOWS.

There were a lot of times, so many times that I would be so close, so, so very close to talking to you and I don't think you knew it. I would get to that point and you'd say, "Well, I guess we're done talking about that." You'd start watching TV and though you told me you we're paying attention I really thought you weren't and nothing would come out. It just wouldn't come out. I know we talked about how easy it is for me to talk myself into things, bad things and so maybe that makes a little more sense to you that way.

I have to tell you, staring at the TV while I am trying to talk to you is rude and no little thing, but they were big things, devastating things to me.

I know that you lose patience and don't understand. I know that sometimes you wanted me to tell you what I was thinking and I didn't because I couldn't. It wasn't because I didn't want to. It was witnessed at the hospital that day in the office with Ramona. I couldn't say the words. My own body is a traitor to what I need to say. Look how far I have come to be able to talk to a cassette.

Sometimes I get so many things going on in my head that I can't recall the original question. It's hard, confusing. When I feel confused, I feel stupid.

I think I'm better at it now, than I was at the hospital. I decided to do it on tape though because we, Ramona and I thought it might be easier. No one will have to sit and wait twenty minutes while I try to take in enough air and courage to get these words out. I can turn off the recorder when I can't talk. I still don't know what you think and I guess that's why I don't know what to expect. It is crucial to me to be able to expect the outcome.

No one can do that without being a mind reader. I don't know what's normal and I want a lot. I need a lot. I have wanted to be first and it made sense to me. I just wanted to be first, the absolute center of your life. I didn't want you to take air without my being there. I didn't want you to live without me being there. I didn't admit it to myself for a long time and I never admitted to anyone, ever, what being first really represented. I was asked that in the hospital. What is first and best? It all boiled down to this. When you have children, they are first, they come first, and they are the center of your life. I mean I have no concept of what it will be like when the kids are gone, but they are the center of your life because they depend on you. Tony asked me in group if I wanted someone to love me so much and pay so much attention to me to make up for all I didn't get or needed. I said no, what a ridiculous thing to say!

The fact is she was right. I would like to be able to say I don't want or need that anymore. Someday I hope I can say it and mean it. I hope I can really say I don't have to be first, I don't have to be the only one. I don't have to be jealous of your life. I guess I am past being jealous about your parents and that's what it's been. I'm jealous of everyone's life. I have all these marvelous friends who have all this love. I want it too!

It's a difficult concept for me. I am trying and there is a little small part that is starting to get it. I love your parents dearly. I think it's important for you to know that I have not understood the concept of "It's the same, but different." There are some things I have to be told. I can't say that I understand it; it isn't something that's ever occurred to me. But then, why would I know that love for your child is different from love of your spouse or your parent. It was never different in my life.

You've talked about wanting to be alone. It's hard for me to understand wanting to be alone, I am terrified of it. You said you wanted to decorate the house the way you wanted to, hang pictures where you wanted them and make messes without worrying about whether someone would be upset with you for it.

All I can say about that is what Ramona and I talked about. I thought that's what I was supposed to be doing to make you happy. It was never a thought or consideration in my head that you might care for me if I didn't do those things. She said it would make no sense for me to know otherwise because I'd had no role models to follow. I thought I was supposed to be cooking, cleaning and finding ways to make the house nice. I knew you didn't like the house and I felt responsible for that. I felt like the places we lived made you unhappy because I wasn't making them nice enough or doing enough for you. I thought I was supposed to do everything for you. It never occurred to me that you might want to decorate it. To be fair, you never told me either.

I don't know if you really are aware what happened with the cleaning. That really escalated with the illness. It was like running in place, trying to do it so perfect that it didn't get done at all. I was going faster and faster getting more and more perfect. My only defense is; I thought that was my place in this life, in your life. If I could do it well we would have a good marriage. If I could cook, clean, garden, create this family setting then you would be happy and all would be well. It didn't have anything to do with me; it had to do with what I could do for you. I'm trying to do all these things and I get frustrated. Ramona tells me it's not frustration, but anger. Anger that it wasn't working and I didn't know what else to do.

I'm still struggling with the definition of depending on each other. I don't have a clear idea of that. It's been explained and talked about till I could scream at my own ignorance. They say it's because I've never let myself depend on anyone. They are right. I've never depended on anyone, for anything. I have taken care of myself and have had a rule, don't let yourself depend on anyone else. In the end there is only myself. It's easier that way. No pain.

My dad always said, "You have to take care of yourself because there is no one else. You come into the world alone, live alone and die alone. He seemed right, I guess it stuck. To depend has meant to lose control over my life. Any small loss and I would die. That's how it feels. They use it against you, hurt you, laugh at you or even hate you. It just hurts too much. I was indoctrinated with these thoughts from birth. It's very much like religion that you are born to. You don't question it too much. It just is.

I have so much to learn. I have a lot to learn, even to be only a friend, and many questions that need answers. In some ways I'm very young and in others very old.

I don't know if anyone realizes just how far I'd gotten or for how long it had been going on before I went into the hospital. I was pretty lost. I know that some memories are distorted. There are things that you did which didn't help. You drank and told me it was because I didn't have dinner ready when you got home. Then you drank and said it was to relax after dinner. I believed it was because I was boring, I bothered you, or that I was no longer attractive.

I don't want to talk about this, I'm not ready. I equated everything to, I must not be doing my job or everyone would be happy. It's not quite that simple. It's a complex situation for me. Sex is complex for me. Sometimes all I really wanted was to be held but I couldn't get one without the other.

I need to talk about being jealous. Ramona and Tony both say it isn't so much jealousy as threat of loss. It's the threat of abandonment with a capital A. It's easy to feel threatened when you don't think very much of yourself. I hate talking to you about it because I can hear you laughing, as you did before. I do feel very threatened.

I'm afraid to call you, afraid to talk to you, afraid to tell you the truth, so I say nothing. I want to. I just can't bring myself to do it. You're not afraid of losing me because I've given you nothing to lose. You told me once before we got married that you had a feeling I was very deep. People say that like it's a compliment. It's not, it's a tragedy.

I don't think you had any idea how deep inside I really was. I know you didn't think you'd have to go to hell and back to find out just how buried I was. God, there are so many things you don't know, that no one knows because I have never said it aloud or written it down to be used against me later. I am saying them here.

I can look at the sun setting and I could cry at the beauty of it. I revel in the destitution and the vastness of a forest untouched by man-kind. I love to sit on the beach and watch the sun set or rise. I love the feel of the wind in my hair right after I wash it. I have never said to anyone that I think humans are fools. If you can just go out where it's just nature all by itself, the way nature made it unblemished by man, there is beauty in the world. I think in the beginning it was too beautiful and man in his arrogance thought he could improve it. God put nature there, he gave us that gift, that art and it's repeated every day in every sunrise and sunset.

I love babies and kids because they represent new, improved and hope of a better future. I love the blunt honesty they have that is un-available with adults. I love to watch them learn and grow. They can be so much better than the rest of us.

I think the most romantic thing in the world would be to be snowed in for two days with wine, cheese and a fireplace. God, don't think I don't know how corny that sounds, but it's true. I hate the color or-ange and my favorite color is rich deep lavender and pink. I really don't mind the color of my eyes at all. The reason I love my dog is that he is the only thing in the world that would love me no matter what.

I've never told anyone that racing horses through a field is like fly-ing, that skiing feels magic, or that I love fur and silk. I've never said, I don't want to feel like an orphan, or that I did. I like houses with lots of plants and wide open space with lots of windows. I like the feel of freshly cut grass beneath my feet, starched cotton shirts and walking at night in the summer. I'm afraid of the dark though so it can't be done alone.

There are other things that aren't very significant. I never tell about those things either because the small things are as dangerous as the big things. I'm told that someday this won't be true and it makes me cry with so wanting it to be true. I'm told that someday I will not feel so alone or so lonely, I cry for that as well because I'm not so sure that it's true.

I like fresh sheets on freshly shaved legs, gray carpet and music. Blues. I regret never having learned to play anything. I always wanted to. I wanted to be an actress or an artist or play music. I wanted to grow up and create something that would outlive me and improve some part of this world.

With the things I've wanted to do and be it must seem odd that I have taken the path I have. I have spent my life trying to compete with men. That competition was important to me, more important than doing what fed my heart. It doesn't seem so important anymore. If something was seen as traditionally male I wanted to do it. I wanted to do it better and faster. Somehow I thought it would make me better than the next female.

I'm just trying to let you know who I really am. It's hard because I'm just beginning to find out myself, and I would like for someone to know.

I'm terrified of the risk, and terrified of not taking the risk. Every time I open my mouth it's a risk. Sometimes I think I'd prefer to shrivel up and die rather that talk about myself.

These things, all these things are difficult for me. To tell you the things that bothered me are not any simpler to get out. It's how I FEEL. Frankly, how I feel is often not how I think. It's in constant conflict as I try to figure out what is true around me.

I care very much. I want everything to be perfect. It has been a panic I can't get past. I don't know if you will understand. I don't come from perfect and I know can't measure up.

THIS IS WHO I AM

Letters

FOLLOWING IS A COLLECTION OF letters I kept over the years. So many letters written and not sent. So many letters written and not received. In therapy, I made wonderful friends in some of the group sessions and some of those letters are included here.

These letters remind me of what my life was like back then and they still help me in my times of need.

March 1988

Dear Dad,

It has taken me a week in the hospital to write to you. I am so broken and no one cares. This is a letter I'm pretty sure not too many parents get. Being a parent myself, I know if I got one like this it would make my blood go cold and probably stop my heart from beating.

Being who you are I doubt you feel any of these things. In some weird way you will feel something, but it won't be right. If you were remotely capable of feeling what you should, I wouldn't be sitting here writing this in the first place. My life would have been vastly different.

For the benefit of your ignorance of my situation, and to enhance your realization of what you and my mother have caused each in your own twisted way, you should know where I am today.

I am in a mental health facility. You will call it the nut house! You would call it the place that they take bug shit crazy people. You will call me one of the crazies! I am a patient. I am trying to get rid of thirty years of baggage, pain, guilt, horror, terror and disgust. I am trying to find out who I am and who I am supposed to be. I am also trying to find out what I am. So far I'm nothing but bits and pieces of other people's life and movies that I admire and try to fit into my life. I try to incorporate all these things into my life that seem to make everyone's life better, including my own, but there is no me.

I have spent my life hiding an existence that so repulsed me, I couldn't face it anywhere, not even in my sleep. I have nightmares that leave me sweating, shivering, exhausted; and when I wake up I can't recall anything but the terror. Let me remind you of a few things Daddy! Let me tell you what it was like to be a little girl in your house. Let me remind you this one and only time. I won't be telling you again. I want you to know and understand, I have not forgotten. I wish I had.

Do you remember, or does it all mean so little to you? Damn it! Do you recall any of it?

Do you remember my imaginary friend Timmy?

I hated you and you'd make me say, "I like this Daddy! This is fun Daddy! I love you Daddy!"

Later I would cry and Timmy would comfort me.

Do you remember down by the little creek?

Do you remember holding my face under the water till God knows why you finally let me out? Do you remember beating me till I couldn't walk straight, then masturbating in my face, sticking things into my little body!?

I don't know why I didn't go insane when I was five years old. Timmy, that figment of my imagination, wanted me to go live with him. I was so afraid of you I didn't go. He would beg me to let him and his family take care of me. I told him no and cried because I couldn't go. At five or six years old I believed you would kill me.

What do you think about? How do you remember this never ending nightmare you have created? Are these memories of your children good for you? Do you smile to yourself and think, 'Ahhh, I love my little girl?'

You made us take off our clothes and crawl around the coffee table, stuck feathers up our rear ends and whacked us with the belt! How did you justify that? How do you remember that? My mother always stuck up for you. I wonder just how she remembers it all, too.

You let Gabe drink that stuff in the garage and beat me because he could have been killed. I believed you when you told me it was my fault he nearly died. Where were you? Why was a 7 year old left in charge of a baby?

I carried that guilt for years. He was not my responsibility. He was yours.

I hope it's true that your life flashes before your eyes as you die and that you feel all the pain and damage you have caused. If I were you I'd worry about just who my maker is.

146

You went to Vietnam for a year and when you came back it started up all over.

I remember the night you came home from Vietnam. You stood in the door way and I truly had no memory of you. I do remember that night well. You were standing in the doorway in your uniform. You were a stranger. I told Mom a salesman is at the door. You were so angry. Right then, that first night you came home, before you even got into the house, the screaming, the beating, the fear, the constant touching, the gifts and my mother's renewed anger over what I got and she did not, started all over. You talked to me like I was your lover. You kept trying to remind me what it was like before you left. You told me you loved me. You told me you missed me and needed me. I pretended I forgot. I thought if I can't remember then it won't happen anymore. I was wrong, wasn't I?

It was worse because I knew what it was like for you to be gone. Life had been bearable for one year. I had friends. I got to go out and play. I went to church. I got to sleep all night. I got to be normal for one year. You just couldn't leave well enough alone could you? You had your chance to leave it alone, leave me alone and live a normal life. YOU, not me, YOU! You threw it away.

Do you think I don't know why we moved so much? You couldn't get caught that way could you? Just leave, move away and get forgotten about. You are slick alright.

I'm only half a person. Christ! Maybe I'm not even a half a person! I have blank spots, holes without memories. Fragments of a thought like broken glass splayed out across the floor? How would you like it if you knew your missing memory was so ugly, so painful you couldn't look at it? How would you like to wake up one day with sick, crazy memories? How would you like to wake up one day and know that you were going insane? I get to do that every damn morning!

Do you remember the empty house next door in North Carolina, the alligators, the snakes, the beatings, the lies and disgusting names, the constant degradation? How about the violent sodomizing of a child, of anyone for that matter? Those are my memories of the fourth grade in North Carolina. What are yours?

"That's what it's like when you grow up so get used to it," you said to me.

Why did you constantly tell me my mother was jealous of me, didn't want me, hated me and blamed me for ruining her life? God, if I close my eyes I can still hear you screaming, "I am your God, I created you and I can destroy you and no one will care. Your mother will be glad. You are mine."

You give me a pair of go-go boots telling me I earned them! You tell Mother you bought them to shut me up. Now she is angry with me. You paid me like a whore. I took them and slept in them. I earned them alright. Maybe I am a whore. I earned them right there in the cornfield in the back of the car when I was nine years old.

Place after place, beating after beating and the repeated raping of a baby's soul, my soul. You raped a baby for sixteen years!

When you lost your legs in that explosion, we got dragged up to that nightmare of a place full of men with missing body parts. There was no warning, no thought about the kids. Just bang! Walk in the door and find fifty men with missing body parts. Act normal! We got bitched at for crying and not being brave. We didn't even know people could survive like that. It was beyond our comprehension.

I was already in shock. I wasn't sure where to look or how to act after walking past that sea of bodies and you ask for a fucking blow job! What is wrong with you? You weren't so drugged that you didn't know what you were doing. You knew enough to get rid of everyone so that you could say it to me. You knew enough to say, "Pull the curtain! Hurry before your mother gets back!"

The worms, your friends, the cigarette burns on my forehead, the knives, the forks, the fireplace poker, the feathers, those books with people fucking animals and the destruction of things I cared about.

Do you have any idea what it was like to lie in bed every night and wonder if someone is coming for you and hear you coming down the hall? There was a dreadful moment of relief that it was finally over. Then there was the fear and disgust a second later. You didn't even sneak. You just came night after night. After a while I guess it didn't matter whether you were coming or not. I'd lie there rock still, listening, as if it would make a difference in what would happen, so tense I would sweat, until I passed out.

If I was awake I would hear, "I'm glad you waited up for me."

It didn't bother you that I cried; you just beat me or got in my face, or put your hands around my throat till I stopped. Now I know it only helped give you your excuse. I was being bad. I was not cooperative. You had to do it if I was bad, right?

I can't stop thinking of all the years and all the scars, inside and out. It was always my fault. You told me once or twice that I was six months old when I started it. How do you justify that? I spent sixteen years of my life raped, beaten savagely and, as a witness to acts that make normal people scream.

I saw you smiling as you choked a puppy to death, then you made us bury it. How many graves did we dig for you?

Then there were the war stories. You laughed about throwing a human being out of a helicopter and making bets to see how high he would bounce!

You would smile while you talk of killing a Vietcong girl my age (10)! You shot her? You thought of me!? Of course I believed you would kill me when you'd laughed about all this death and killing. You told me you would kill me if you felt like it and no one would know or care so many times. I feel bad when I tell my kids I am going to punish them for something.

You laughed about throwing "gooks" out of airplanes! It doesn't even matter if it's true or not. What kind of monster says that to his child? You do! I want to scream and scream and scream and never stop! But, I can't! No one will hear me and who the hell in their right mind would believe me? Who can I really tell all this to that will not look at me with disgust, or accuse me of lying? You ass! My husband says all he can see when he looks at me is what happened to me. He doesn't know the tip of the iceberg.

You were right when you told me, "Who the fuck will believe you?

I'm a war hero."

I get to call you Daddy.

I was miserable, unhappy and desperately terrified as a kid. I have nothing I can compare it to. I woke up in the morning to worry when it would all start. Sometimes I actually woke up hoping the beating and the screaming would start early and be over. Sometimes the tension of waiting was more than I could take. I went to sleep petrified of what would happen in the night. I woke up worrying terrified of what would happen in the day.

When I got the opportunity I would tell you I was spending the night at some friend's house, then hide and sleep in the closet of my room.

It was rare that I was allowed out as you told me, "You are a whore, a thief, a trouble maker and a cunt! You cannot really expect to be allowed in the homes of nice people. Decent people don't want trash like you bothering them or especially staying in their homes."

I prayed every day to a God who never answered until one day I decided He didn't care either. I must have done something really awful to deserve this. Christian folks are always telling me that God answers prayers and helps people. Why would God save you, let you live through that explosion, and not save me? How come you got to ask God to live? Why won't he let me die?

There are so many things I haven't written and there isn't enough paper anyway. I am thirty-three years old. I hate you. I hate you so much my blood hurts as it passes through the veins of my arms. I have thought about when I get out of here and I think I will probably hunt you down and kill you. Then I will sit, no matter how long it takes, and watch your flesh rot and melt into the dirt of some trash heap so you can't hurt anyone any more. So you can't hurt me anymore.

YOU DELIGHT IN SAYING I AM JUST LIKE YOU! I AM NOTHING LIKE YOU AND I AM DEEPLY OFFENDED EVERY TIME YOU SAY IT!!

I WANT TO CUT MYSELF SO ALL OF YOUR BLOOD GETS OUT OF ME!

Your filthy language, your constant dirty jokes and stories of what you do to and with women is disgusting. I don't want you around my children. The stakes are too high. You are a great risk to them and they deserve better. If you call I won't come to the phone and you are not to talk to my daughters. If you try to call I will have the number changed and unlisted. If you come to town we will not see you. If you come to my house I will call the police and have you removed. If you come back after that I will shoot you myself!

I DON'T HAVE TO PUT UP WITH YOU ANYMORE.

This is not an ugly fight with you, it's just the end. I can't afford you anymore. I'm not going to lie about you or for you anymore. If I am asked about my father I will simply say that I don't have one. I can say that because you see, I never really did. You are nothing but a God damn sperm donor to freaking egg donor! I hope you aren't ruining anyone else's life as you have nearly ruined mine. They tell me something must have happened in your life to make you the way you are. I don't know and at this point I don't care what happened to you! Everyone has choices. Everyone! You chose to live a decadent, selfish, thieving, deviant, sick, perverted, pedophile, child molesting demented and self-serving life. You feed off other people.

I also have a choice. I choose to somehow live, to be happy, and to get on with it, to find out who I am and was supposed to be instead of this miserable pretend person that I grew into.

I am going to be OK, but because of me, in spite of you.

Annie

June 1988

Dear Mother,

I guess I should stop saying I won't be writing any more letters to you. I say it, and I mean it, then I write another one.

I've tried hard to reconcile the fact that you and Dad are quite crazy and neither of you even gets it!

Bits and pieces of information float through my head here and there, but nothing of consequence. I try to think what you look like. It takes considerable effort to think of anything but your nicotine stained teeth and your bright red mouth.

I nearly sent back the card you sent my daughter for her birthday. I couldn't decide why she shouldn't have it so I gave it to her. I can't do anything till I decide why I'm doing it. I am through just doing things out of some reaction I don't understand.

Do I want to hurt you or save myself? Maybe it's a little of both or neither. I don't know so the card stayed here… this time.

Why don't you write me? I keep thinking there will be a card or letter today, but there is never a today that it happens. Every day I have to remind myself that's what there's always been, nothing. So can you tell me why I keep hoping and looking?

Don't you wonder what has happened to me over the last three months?

Friends and family have slipped away from me. I'm an embarrassment. I shouldn't be the embarrassment, you should! Somehow you gave me all those rotten feelings that don't belong to me. I try hard to wash the dirt away but I'm clumsy with the wash rag.

A lot has happened in the last three months but I guess you don't care to hear about it. Don't worry. It's a sin to be that rude to your parents. Don't bore them, bother them or upset them. Don't open your mouth and don't have an opinion that hasn't been handed down by one of them. And for Christ's sake don't ask for any help!

Yes, I'm bitter. I don't want you to think I don't realize it. I can just see you going and getting your cheap wine and your fancy glass.

Does it make you numb the way drugs did for me? I won't ever know will I? I wish you've lost as much sleep as I have, but I know you have not.

Annie

December 1988

Hello Mother,

Thought I would send a thank you for the Christmas gifts and enclose it along with the notes the kids wrote. I was a little surprised to hear from you after the letter I sent you.

It's been a difficult year for me and I work hard every day at keeping myself together. The depression is a constant problem that I constantly try to fight off. I take antidepressants and at times wonder why. I've only been taking them for about a month, the doctor is pleased and so is the therapist, so I guess I'm where I should be. They make me feel thick and slow.

I got married again. I have to admit I have found myself embarrassed to be announcing yet another. It was a real wedding, complete with a gown and cake, etc. He has never been married and wanted to do it right. His father gave me away. I just want to be happy.

I'm not working now. I was fired from my last job, yet another consequence of my hospitalization. I saw an attorney and seriously considered suing, but decided not to. I am trying to get on with my life and didn't want to get hung up in a long, drawn-out lawsuit.

Alaska is beautiful. We've seen the northern lights a couple of times. It's truly a remarkable sight. Both girls are impressed. Nice thing about being married to a pilot is get to fly around the area and have seen glaciers both from the ground and the air. We see moose in town all the time right in our yard!

Annie

November 1988

Hi Annie,

It's great to hear from you! I miss you too! You make Alaska sound really beautiful. I'm glad you like it.

Group talks about you all the time, (all good stuff of course). Mike and I think you're a really great example of someone with the courage to pull it together and to use your therapy to the fullest advantage. You should be proud of yourself for all the good work you've done so far. I think the last time I saw you I didn't really say how much I appreciate you. Working with you reminds me of why I'm in the business!

Always remember, Dad is not ten feet tall, he only has fake tall legs and you are no longer a child. You're a mature woman who is as powerful now as he ever was (and no longer is). Hold onto this. Sounds like you're doing what you can to get your support system into place and once you get that, your anxiety will ease up. Try physical activity, (aerobics, etc.) and relaxation exercises should help.

Things are good with me, my private practice is building up slowly and I love being my own boss. RJ and I are getting along great. We went to his sister's in San Diego for Thanksgiving - it was fun. His family is coming to our place for Christmas and of course I want it to be perfect! Oh well, what they see is what they get! I have to remember to have fun for me too and not go crazy doing everything for everybody.

I bet you'll have a beautiful white Christmas where you are. It must be like living in a postcard! I'm glad you say your kids are happy, now make yourself happy. You're free to do that you know! HA HA!! Whatever you do take good care of yourself!

Love Tony (my first group therapist during my hospital stay).

December 1988

Dear Tina,

I'm finally into a group. It's different from the group you and I went to together. We have an Acting Therapist to run the group instead of a certified one. I'm not sure I like that. I guess I'll try it for a while anyway. It bothers me to think that someone is messing with my head that isn't qualified. I think I need more than I'll be getting from this. There are other groups available, but the waiting list is very long. Some told me there is as long as one year wait list. It's better than nothing I suppose.

I finally found a therapist!

I'm calmer. She thinks I should be on meds. She swears it's not addictive and I'll only be on them for 6 months. I don't know how I feel about that. We have talked about what's going on with me. Well, I don't know if you can call it talking. It's hardly conversational. She doesn't say much. I wish she would. She writes notes like crazy and looks serene. Sometimes she sits behind me. I don't like that. Feels like I am being stalked. It makes me feel like I need to say really important, profound things. She hardly even looks at me. I will give it a couple of months and see if it improves.

I've been having such a hard time with the craziness coming back. I am not breaking things, but the nightmares, the adrenaline rushes and the shakes.

Living here is very different from anything and anywhere I have ever lived. There are very few reminders of the past. The only time I recall living in snow at all was the year my father was overseas and my family stayed in Massachusetts. It was the best year of my childhood.

Elaine (new therapist) says maybe I feel safe here and that it allows for things to come up for me again. I dream like crazy and the dreams feel crazy too. I have to admit the medication is beginning to help me to stay asleep, but that's all. I still dream. I wish I wouldn't. The bags under my eyes are going away.

I didn't realize I would lose so much when I left Nevada. I lost my friends, my therapist, and my new goals. I lost a whole support system that I'd so carefully and cautiously put together. You all became my family and understood me. Now I find myself trying to rebuild all that and it's difficult. I really do miss you all so much.

I've gone on and on. There is an upside to life. I might have to put on magnifying glasses to see it, but there is. I guess I could tell you about that instead of all this gloom and doom.

Still planning on school in January and trying to get ready for the holidays. I got a nice letter from Tony. It was encouraging and I was so glad to hear from her. She is a very special lady. I hope that the group realizes how lucky they are to have her. I have discovered there are some real flakes out there, and some are pretty insensitive to boot.

Take care, I know you don't do Christmas but I hope the holiday is good for you anyway.

Write soon, Love Annie

December 1988

Dear Tony,

I went to my first group last night. I was nervous and irritable. I don't know how anyone puts up with me. I've been having a difficult time.

How do you tell someone you're feeling weak and becoming invisible? I can't explain the screaming in the middle of the night. I am lonely for someone to understand who I am. I'm afraid I've lost more ground than anyone can imagine. How do you tell someone this all seems endless and it makes me afraid? I'm tired. I thought it was over and it's not. I'm maintaining on the outside, smiling in the right places and telling the right jokes, but inside I'm a tornado of turmoil. I'm afraid that in the end I will be alone because I didn't really matter. All these months gone by and it's back. The blackness is here. I'm not good enough for anyone to want me to stay, or for them to stay. I remember what you said one day. Fake it till you make it. I am.

My mother sent Christmas gifts. I cried for over an hour and was never sure why. I wanted a letter, a card, something. There was none. It served as another reminder to me that she didn't care. I was again that little girl with a broken heart. I was also angry with myself because I thought I was done crying over her. I wrote her that letter. I wrote her off and out of my life. I did that, damn it and there I was crying my heart out over her. I wanted some proof of her love and a gift wasn't it. I can't ask her for it, she has to give it because she wants to, not because I asked, but what "it" is I don't know. It's empty if I have to give her the words. I cried till I wore myself out. No one in the house knew what to do.

I did tell everyone if anything came from my father it was to be sent back. I'm fighting to get myself back together. I've got to get myself back together. I put a note back into my pocket. It says: 'Just make it through this moment, you will then be OK'. I'm back to counting moments instead of minutes.

Love Annie

December 23, 1988

Annie,

It's hard for me to write. When you left, (in fact, that day), I sat down and wrote you a letter. It didn't really say what I wanted it to and obviously I never mailed it. I want you to somehow understand how much you meant (and mean) to me. I once said that we could be friends and I believe that. I hope we will be much more than that.

I care for you. I care how you are, what you feel and if you're happy. I know that we've begun very different lives. And I know that it's probably the best thing that could happen. I want you to know that I am here for you, if you need something that I can give, please, be sure to ask.

You're an amazing person. I respect you and love you very much. I know that you will do great things in your life. You have overcome tremendous obstacles and maybe that will help you in the years to come.

I would also like Holly and Emily to know that I love them, I will leave that up to you. I don't want to interfere or disrupt their lives, but I hope they know how much I care.

I don't really know what else to say. I think about you a lot. Sometimes it makes me feel happy, sometimes sad. Please keep in touch with me.

I sincerely wish you Merry Christmas and all the happiness in the world. I hope to be hearing from you.

Love David, (ex-husband)

December 26, 1988

Dear David,

I got your letter a couple of days ago and have been thinking about it ever since. It makes me sad to think about 'us'. I'm still struggling with the same old questions. Maybe I'll never know and must find peace in knowing that I'll be alone. I can't find that middle ground, or the gray that is supposed to be so wonderful. I have not been happy. I smile and I do and say the right things but inside, I'm dying.

Therapy and group has become a struggle for me to get through. I feel things that I'm desperately trying to fight off. The new doctor and therapist are saying good, go with it, feel it. They don't want me fighting it off, they say fighting it off keeps me sick. They want me to feel it and be done with it. It doesn't seem very constructive to me though. I don't feel like I have much control over it anyway. I've been on antidepressants for a month. I'm not convinced they help much. I sleep better and have stopped shaking constantly but that's about it. I feel lethargic, sluggish. Every time I complain to the doctor he increases the dosage.

I think about what has happened since I left Vegas a lot. I wanted a clean start and I sure got one by God. I did not anticipate, (nor did anyone else) the loneliness of that decision. I feel pretty alone here.

I think of you often. I didn't write because I wasn't sure you would want me to. I feared I would be an intrusion into your new life and really don't want to be.

Since you mentioned it in your letter I have to mention that Holly and Emily have been a bit ambivalent about you. They missed you and felt like you weren't interested. A lot has happened in the last year that will take years for them to understand, if they ever can. It hasn't much mattered what I have to say about it right now, I think that time and age will put things into perspective for them eventually.

We especially missed Thanksgiving this year. It seemed so quiet. We missed the love and the gaiety of your family and all the kids. I find myself crying as I write this. So much was lost, so much seems unattainable to me. I try so hard. I miss your family a lot.

Good grief, I really do go on. That's enough of that! It really isn't all gloom and doom. We learned how to cross country ski and are hooked. Emily, of course, wants to race and loves it when we come to a hill. Holly just likes to get a steady pace going. It's very beautiful here.

I guess that's about all I have to tell you about. You matter a lot to me, too. There have been times when I wish things could have been different, but I know, for me at least, they couldn't really have gone any other way. Isn't hindsight a wonderful thing? I suppose it's little consolation for you to know that it would have ended the same for me no matter who it was. They say life goes on, I guess it does, whether we like it or not. I hope your Christmas was good and you enjoyed your kids. I hope you will send them my love. Christmas here was nice, very white, as it snowed, very beautiful and quite traditional. It's like living in a postcard.

Please write, I guess I still think that you might not though I know there isn't any reason to think that way.

Love Annie

January 1989

Dear Juanita,

I don't know where the time has gone. I started at UAA and have been busy ever since. Had exams last week and the week before. Have a biology class that is kicking my, well you can fill in the blank there. It's an interesting but tough class. I had to take a lab with it and joy of joys; I will be cutting up a pig in about two weeks. Stay tuned I will let you know if I make it without passing out cold onto an even colder floor.

My birthday came and went; funny they don't generate the excuse for a party that they used to. I must be getting old whether I like it or not. Got flowers and we went to dinner and a movie. Saw Rainman. I really liked it. Been sticking pretty close to home with the weather as cold as it is. It's terrible, though it seems to be improving. I have discovered the true meaning of cabin fever over the last three weeks. When you go outside for even a short time your eyelashes freeze and so do your nose hairs when you breathe. Sooooo, we stay in. Even the dog is bored.

I finally found a therapist I can settle down with. I can't believe how hard it's been to find someone I can work with. Carol seems to be pretty creative and we've been doing some real neat things. Some of its pretty emotional, some of it not, just like therapy eh? I finally feel as though I'm making some progress though, however small it may be. I guess I'm feeling better about many things. The last couple of months have been hard on me, progress or not.

I need to go and study Biology. It's what I live for lately.

Write soon, Love Annie

May 1989

Dear Princess,

Thank you for such sweet thoughts of me, honey. Uncle Clay won't ever run out of hugs and kisses for you. I'm glad you have that little island of memory of me as a cushion for yourself.

Don't be afraid to tell me anything honey. I'll guard it with my soul. I won't even tell God without your approval.

I know better than anyone how ill my brother Bryan is. We were both abused as kids ourselves. For that same reason I have a better understanding of your own emptiness, loneliness, insecurity and doubts about your self-worth. Bryan's total lifetime has been one of utter hell and fear and insecurity and self-doubt. He has devoted all his life, all his waking hours, to try to make people think that he is great because he has always had such a low opinion of himself, due to being abused. Over the years, like a cancer this has spread through his awareness and ruined his life. You can't hate diarrhea out of your body, you can get rid of it with a positive approach.

I can see that this is going to take a huge amount of writing for us to get all out thoughts out on paper, so I hope you keep writing to me.

I have never taken anything seriously that your father or mother has ever said. I understand their condition. Kate had been too adversely affected by Bryan. I did however believe that he had indoctrinated all of you kids into thinking that I was a lot worse and he was a lot better. That's why I stayed off at a distance, to reduce the conflict. There wasn't much opportunity to express my viewpoint so I thought it was best to just let you all grow up. Considering John's stomach problems and isolation I am beginning to think the problem is worse than I imagined. Eventually you may have to give a lot of yourself to help John improve his life.

I was at Bryan's graduation down in San Diego along with your father and his wife. Bryan looked great. I even got a lump in my throat. It's a shame, every time Bryan would brag about something he was proud of in training your father would smother him out with a bigger, better story.

When I was very young, and was living with my hated stepmother, I got a lot of security and a feeling of safety from knowing that my Aunt Irene was my Godmother. All I needed to help me feel warm, safe, secure and loved was to know that I had my Godmother Aunt Irene who loved me like crazy no matter what I did. Just like I love you. Anyway it's a real title when you get to stand up for someone who is being baptized in a Christian church. Aunt Irene didn't even have to be there, someone represented her by proxy. Although I'm not a Christian (probably more of a Jewish faith) I don't think that would matter much if you wanted me to be your Godfather. Think about it.

In many ways Santa Claus and the Easter Bunny are real, and so is your crown, Old Uncle Clay keeps it locked up in his heart for you.

Love is hard to get rid of, the more you give it away, the more you end up with.

XXXXOOOO, Your Uncle Clay

June 1989

Dear Mother,

I think I should be polite. I'm saying goodbye. In saying it, I fear I'm giving up more than my mother. It means I am giving up hope on you. I give up what shred of family I have left. I'm worried about it and I'm not sure why. All I really have are tattered shreds of a fantasy and hope.

I'm trying to tell you that you blew it for the last time. I always hope, and somehow manage to believe you'll be there for me. You never are and I get hurt over and over and over. I don't want to be hurt anymore. There are just too many times that you haven't been there for me. You are my mother! If I were to die tomorrow, would you even bother to come the funeral? I think not. You haven't attended any of my marriages or my graduations. You helped beat me. You beat me on your own. You dragged me over to Dad!

You haven't tried to have any kind of relationship with your grandchildren or with me. I had emergency surgery and begged you to come, you didn't. My oldest daughter was badly injured when she was hit by a car and you didn't come. When I was small and defenseless you didn't come. Goddamn it! You never show up!

I am finished waiting for you to show up. I realize I won't be much of a loss in your life, and oddly enough you won't be much of a loss in mine either. You've never really existed have you? The fantasy will be a great loss but I'm assured something healthy and honest will replace it. I've been talking with my counselor about how you can't miss something you never really had, but it did feel real to me. It's all I have. The hope was real. The pain was real, is real.

I don't want to hurt anymore.

Annie

June 1989

Annie Honey,

Grandma called and said she had a great time? She sounded like she meant it. Try not to let your feelings about grandma bother you. I get the same treatment from her. She loves (and needs) to make mountains out of sesame seeds. That sort of behavior puts pressure on anybody. Communicate to me anyway you want, in your own way, on your own terms, anytime you feel comfortable about it. I understand a little about how you feel, honey bunch. I'm going to be around for about another 45 years so take your time and be comfortable about waiting. Besides, letter writing gives you more time to gather your thoughts.

I'm sure your brother Bryan would like to hear from you, but don't give him your address right away if you prefer that your father doesn't get it. Bryan Sr. has always picked through other peoples private belongings and taken what he wanted. That seems to include just about everyone in the family. Your father has always been considered not quite trustworthy by anyone in the family, even less so in later years. Mostly he's just humored and tolerated. Brother Bryan will discover this eventually.

I love you honey, Uncle Clay

July 1989

Dear Mother,

This letter is death of a fantasy and death of hope built on fantasy. It is death of my struggle with life as it pertains to you. Writing to you and telling you what I feel means I really have given it up. Telling you what I want cuts off the cancer that consumes me.

You're guilty of the abuse too. Where were you when I was just a little child? Was I ever really a little small baby girl? Look at the photos. In the few I have the eyes are sad. My childhood was taken from me. Did you ever say you were sorry? NO! Have you bothered to say to anyone, much less me, how is she doing? Is she any better? NO! You don't even ask about me. The guilt is not mine. It's yours! TAKE IT!

The pain is mine. The struggle is mine. This life today that I muddle through is mine. I am a mess. I cry myself to sleep at night. I can't get close to anyone. I cry for my mother like a five year old. I am so lost.

I tried to be a good daughter. I tried to make you love me. I needed a mother so badly and didn't have one. I don't have one. You gave birth to me and for as long as I can remember it was a constant struggle to find a key to your heart. There is no key.

You allowed what went on in all those houses. You dragged us to him. Didn't you ever think it was odd that my brothers would have to beat me with my clothes off? Don't you ever think it was excessive to drag me around by my hair, to put cigarettes out on my forehead, to spit in my face, and to think you had to compete with me for your husband?

Annie

June 1989

Hello Sugar,

Got your letter June first, just before my birthday. Thank you for my beautiful painting, I'll treasure it always. There seems to be a lot of you in it. A lot of beauty, a dreamy cozy safe place, and a hauntingly empty loneliness. It's beautiful honey, I'll keep it close to my heart.

I want you to know (regarding your letter, about why I didn't rescue you from that ugliness) my heart aches at remembering those days. I know very well how (my brother) Bryan always made himself look good and made me look bad. He has done that defensively all his life. Based on that, I thought that he was just a lousy parent with a rotten streak in him. I was convinced that with his lies and weaknesses that he had convinced you kids that I was a real bad character and he was a much better guy. It hurt me because it prevented your brothers, you and myself from being close. I thought that I had to live with that situation since I couldn't compete against the lies when I saw you guys so seldom. I thought that I might only confuse you with the truth after you had spent a lifetime with his selfish bullshit. I didn't know of the real ugly things he did to you. Had I known that I would have tried to take legal action against him.

I remember one time specifically, (typical of many other times) when Bryan had opened that store in Eureka for sales of his junk and you were supposed to work there, pretty much alone, all day, to sell to the tourists. I was across the street (in a coffee shop) with Bryan and we sort of said hello and waved, but the apprehensive look on your face, seemed to me to say, he's kind of a creep and it's best to stay away. I wanted more than anything to hug you and let you know how lucky I was to be your uncle and how much I cared for you. It was like being stabbed in the heart. I know now many years later, your look was a different kind of hurt. On the other hand, I have my little girl back. XXOO. Forever.

I am your Godfather. Bryan had told me that he had you baptized and someone had stood in for me by proxy. I understand your point on religion, but I'm glad I'm your uncle and Godfather also.

Write to John once in a while. To let him know you care about him. Not to advise him or anything. Just to let him have a chance to get close to you. Just give to each other, don't take. As the years go by you will be a great comfort to each other.

Bryan did seem pleased that you had written to him (in Saudi), he mentioned it several times over the weekend. I would almost say he seemed proud of it, though he probably wouldn't admit it. It's not the popular thing to do.

Promise you'll keep on writing to me honey, even if the letters are far apart. Send a postcard at least.

Hugs and kisses, Your loving Uncle Clay

November 1989

Dear Uncle Clay,

Thought that I had better get to this letter. I been telling myself for weeks that I had to get this letter to you and just haven't had any time between my schedule and the kids.

I hear that my dad had a stroke. I guess that he is getting up there now and life has not been easy for him these days. There is a social worker that keeps tabs on him. They watch his involvement with women who have kids. I feel a little sorry for him I guess. It isn't very often that anyone ever tells him he is wrong and then makes him live with it. I think that is the right thing to do, but I do think that it's hard on him and he is my father after all. I guess I just get soft every once in a while. I know that he must have a lot of problems of his own and I feel bad for that. It doesn't change anything for me though. Maybe this is justice in a roundabout way. I write Bryan about every other month in Desert Storm. I try to write more than that but am never sure if I should or not. He still doesn't have my address. I just write and hope that he is doing well and happy. I know it is probably hard for him to be so far away, but I do think that it will grow him up a whole lot.

Haven't heard from Gabe in a little while. His wife gets mad if he runs up the phone and we call him once in a while. He is a great kid. He has a settled life with Sarah and has direction and all. He really has come a long way since the oil fields in Texas. He misses the girls like crazy and they miss him. Uncle Gabe is very special. I wouldn't want it to get out but I do feel closer to Gabe, always have, he is very special to me too. Don't worry, we are in touch. My therapy with Carol is going very well. I guess that it should as I try really hard. She tells me that she is very happy with me.

The holidays are a little rough for me to get through. Always have been. I want so much for them to be special and try so hard to make them that way that I end up driving everyone around me nuts. We are working on that these days, among other things. If you do decide to come up it would be great for you to come in and meet her with me.

I know that she looks at it as a very special opportunity to meet other members of the family and has said that it rarely happens but when it does you get more insight and can help her client (me) much better. She is great and I would like you to meet her and vice versa. Don't be worrying about me too much, I am in good hands.

I get a little down lately (it's easy to do here in the winter) but I am doing OK. I may even be off this medication in the spring. Dr. G. was thinking about taking me off of it in January but decided to leave well enough alone for a little while. I guess that I look at going off the meds as a kind of graduation into life. Sometimes I get a little afraid that I won't be able to deal with things without it. She says not to worry right now. So I don't think about it much. I just know that the anti-depressants have helped me a great deal. This is probably the most normal year I have ever had and the most peaceful. Even the kids have mentioned how calm I manage to stay.

One of my goals in therapy has been to improve and learn coping skills that aren't destructive and I have done a pretty good job. I am feeling kind of pleased with myself can you tell? Give Aunt Kerry and the boys my love. Hope that you enjoy the photos, just sorry that it took so long to get them to you. Write soon, I love you,

Annie

November 1989

Dear Annie,

Great surprise to me, the other night, Gabe called from Vegas and we talked for about an hour and a half. I can't tell you how great it was to hear from him. He is going to be in a bike race in Riverside and will be over to see us. I'm sure you know how wonderful it can be to hear from someone you thought wasn't aware you existed. He sounded so aware and bright, like he really had his shit together. Sounds like he has a good job and plans ahead of him. Can't wait to see him. I would like to get to know your counselor someday if you felt OK about it. I won't do anything you don't want so don't be concerned about it. Just give it some thought. I feel so helpless down here not knowing more about things.

How about trading me some hugs and kisses for the holidays, here is mine: XOXOXOXOXOX

Love You! Uncle Clay

June 1991

Dear Annie,

I understand your father moved out from Jill's and is living near the beach. Bryan is finished with his leave and is back down on the base. He is about to leave for Okinawa and vicinity for a year. Jill visited Gabe in Las Vegas recently; I understand things are going well there.

Weather has been a lot more pleasant this month than I expected. Less than 100 during the day and cool in the evenings. I generally hate summers here. I'm a cool weather type of person.

Uncle Clay

January 1, 1992

Dear Ramona,

I have thought about you so often since I left Las Vegas, and it was such a treat for me to talk to you on the phone a few months ago. I have wanted to write and tell you about it but I find myself so busy it's hard to find time.

Carol and I talked about it too because you had been such an authority figure for me. I depended on you so much that I had left you up there on the pedestal and didn't seem to be able to make you quite human. You were so very much more than that to me. I am assuming you are aware of that, though. Although I admit to working very hard to get my life together, you were an intricate part and I couldn't have begun it nor done it alone. I guess I just want to tell you thanks for that. I also want to tell you that talking to you on the phone after all this time was freeing for me. I discovered I could talk to you without feeling like the inept little girl that I felt I was when I first saw you. It was wonderful.

I'm not the same person that's for sure. I even called the social worker who took that phone call when I turned in my father. I talked to her about what it meant to me when she called me when I got home from the hospital. She told me what she had been doing over the last couple of years and I thought you might be interested.

My father can't be brought up on any charges as he seems to have squirmed out of them. She goes out, introduces herself and tells them about my letter, past allegations, etc., gives her card to the woman and to the children. There are always children. She tells them to call if they need her. Dear old Daddy isn't keeping many girlfriends these days. It isn't quite the kind of justice I'd been hoping for but knowing how my father is I am sure it bothers the hell out of him that someone is telling him, "No… you can't do this and we are watching you." I have to admit it's better than nothing. This woman made it her personal interest, I admire her for that.

Good grief I am rambling and I hate it when I do that. Seems I have much to say and no words. The bottom line here is, I am at peace, I am happy, and I have accepted who I am with all my baggage good and bad, most of the time.

I've enclosed a copy of a newspaper that came out in Eagle River. It was quite exciting. I think the article was well done, and thought you'd enjoy it. I am quite proud that because of my story coming out like that the editor did a whole series on child abuse. She wrote about how to recognize, what to do, who to call etc.

Affectionately, Annie

AFFIRMATIONS

My reaction to an emotional situation is just my opinion; it is not necessarily the truth.

I can become happy and free by deciding to leave the world and those in it alone and concentrate on myself instead.

I am peaceful, I am happy, I am capable, I am creative.

I am loved, I am lovable.

I am caring, I am free, I am forgiven.

I try hard, I am pretty, I am healthy.

I am intelligent, I am neat, I am honest.

I am trustworthy, I am peaceful.

I am loving, I am fun, I am strong.

I am athletic, I am a winner, I am a survivor.

I am a good mother, I am a good friend.

I am logical, I am sensitive.

I am getting better, I work on me, I am smart.

I can love, I can love me.

I can be myself, I am artistic.

I am trying to find me and me is going to be OK.

I am what I am, not perfect, not all knowing, be happy with that.

You must walk the path to get to your goals.

Today is part of life's curriculum, learn it and tomorrow will take care of itself.

You don't really know me, so your opinion of me is questionable.

I'm better than you think.

I'm better than I think.

Think of this, if you have made it through life with what you know so far, it is obvious that you will make it through the rest of your life once you possess a greater knowledge.

Maybe all that I have to do is look at this differently.

What is the underlying emotion or opinion here?

Am I creating struggle?

Head toward your goal, even if it seems a long way off.

Nothing and no one will carry you. You will have to carry yourself.

Whose voice do you hear in your head telling you ugly things?

By trying to maintain total control, you have none.

Once you accept that you are the cause of your present struggle, you can then know that it can be eliminated.

I am having a normal reaction to an abnormal situation in my past.

When all else seems to fail, my dog loves me.

Defeat lies not in failing or making mistakes; rather, it lies in giving up on ourselves when we do so.

What others think of you is not important. They don't have all the facts.

What others think of you is not important. They don't have all the facts.

Yes, I wrote that twice on purpose. It's an important one to me.

When something bad happens you have choices.
Let it define you.
Let it destroy you.
Let it make you strong.

Part Three – Redemption

Can You Hear Me Now?

Almost Over

SPRING WILL BE HERE SOON, I muse to myself as I enjoy a quiet minute before the bus comes and drops off my starving kids. There's been a moose in the yard all afternoon but she and her baby have wandered off now.

I've been living in Alaska for nearly ten years. I love the remoteness: it appeals to my need to feel safe. No one just shows up in the state of Alaska. Only my best of friends have come up here. The scenery is beautiful. Winter or summer, there is no such thing as a bad view. There's an explosion of green when summer races in for its short tenure and a wash of whites and grays as the long winter descends.

I have remarried and we have a houseful of kids to raise; his four and my three. I have dairy goats that I breed, sell and show. We raise a couple of turkeys every year that always get named Christmas and Thanksgiving. We want the kids to remember we will be putting them into the freezer. A pig named Porkchop lives in the back corner of the property. I call this my 'Davey Crockett Period'. I have learned to make soap, raise a sheep and spin his wool into yarn and then knit a sweater. I make cheese from all the goat milk. I bake and cook every day. We fish all summer and I smoke the salmon. I feel safe and content.

I am forty-three years old and have spent twenty years searching for who I am and confronting the demons of my childhood. I have made the same mistakes over and over. I fell apart. I put myself back together again. I am nearing the end of ten years of therapy and group counseling. I still have nightmares, but they don't take the air out of me like they used to. Life has become manageable. It's more than I ever dared to hope for.

I think to myself that I should call my mother this week. I sigh. I call my mother once a month. I have managed to find a way to set aside my feelings about her parenting skills. I have made a conscious effort to accept the few maternal crumbs she tosses my way. I have come to the point where I am willing to look the other way, maybe forgive. I don't think she wants to see me. We've offered to buy tickets several times for her and her husband, but there is always an excuse to not make the trip. We talk about her garden, her yard and her neighbor that she doesn't like much. I talk about my life and the kids, but it is always clear she isn't interested. I cling to the idea, the hope, that a relationship may be possible given some more time. As the kids get older, it is more difficult to get them on the phone with her. They don't know her and she makes little effort. The worst part of our talks is that she martyrs herself. Her kids don't pay enough attention, they don't visit, everyone's angry and she doesn't understand why. She isn't sorry for anything because it's not her fault. I think about all of this. I groan to myself; I don't think I'll call her this week.

The phone rings loudly in the quiet of the house and startles me.

"Hello, hello?" Dead air. "Who is this?"

"Hey, it's me." I recognize my brother John's voice. There's a bad connection and he can't hear me. He'll call me back.

I sit at the table, looking at a magazine to kill some time. He never calls this time of day, so I am curious and I hope he calls quickly before the chaos of after-school activity begins. The phone finally rings again. I get up and lean against the counter to talk to him.

"What's up?"

"Wow! That's better," he says.

I can hear him sucking in a deep breath, "Well..." He pauses, "Dad's dying."

"Really!" It's a statement, not a question. I don't know what to make of this. I feel strangely unaffected.

It's been ten years since I have had any contact with my father: no letters, cards or phone calls. I made that decision and it has been a good one. Now, I don't know what to think or say. I don't feel or think any of the things I thought I would or should. I'm confused.

I should feel bad.

I should cry.

I should feel anything besides this ghoulish glee that is beginning to spread slowly and take over my body!

Should. This word is supposed to be banned from my vocabulary, yet here I am. Should, should, should!

What kind of person am I? I have the fleeting thought that I am a bad person and it catches me off guard. For a moment, I am that little girl who is bad, selfish and undeserving.

My heart is pounding so hard my chest hurts. There's a cold sweat starting on my forehead accompanied by a queasy stomach. My knees feel weak and I sit at the dining table.

In a flash I recall the pain of the last twenty years, the letters I wrote that he laughed at. The hospital stay. Two years on disability. The failures of my too many marriages. The inadequacy I've felt in raising my children. My head is spinning with the knowledge of a life stolen from me. A life that others take for granted, I have to fight for, fake and maybe never have at all.

I have self-talk for these times and I force it to my consciousness since my brain has gone into hyper-speed. When I question my thinking, like I'm doing now, there is a couple of questions I ask myself that have never failed me. First, where is the proof? Second, how long will this thought or situation matter?

My thought is: I'm a bad person. So, I start with the first question: where is the proof? Well, it's in the fact that I am exhilarated that someone is going to die!

My thoughts drift to the second question: is this going to matter in fifteen minutes? YES! A day? YES! A week, month, year, decade? YES! YES! YES! YES!

I am caught in a wind tunnel and continue berating myself soundly and uselessly. What kind of person am I? Hmph, I've been asking myself that question my whole life and here it is again. I want to scream and break things because I can't get the voices out of my head.

Carol is my therapist. She's so dear to me. I hear her asking, "Whose voice do you hear calling you those things?" It's my father's and my mother's voices. Old noise.

John is still talking. I've nearly forgotten I was talking to him. He says something about Dad doesn't really want me there, and that he called me a whore. This is what my father thinks about as he lay dying. Are you kidding me? I am at the same time mystified and disgusted.

"Yeah, I don't know if there is time for you to get there." Then he asks, "Jesus! Why do you want to be there after he called you names like that?"

"What?" I exclaim. "I have to be there! What do you mean there's not time for me to get there? What's wrong with him? Are you going to go?"

I don't hear any of his answers.

I can't wait to get off the phone and pack. It's like Christmas, Easter, and my birthday all in one day. The angels must be singing. He's dying! I will see him to hell. I am euphoric! Driven! Elated! I must be there to see it for myself.

The pounding in my chest hurts. I can almost hear the blood rushing through my body. It's hard to concentrate and I have to ask again. I realize I am not giving him time to answer as I shoot questions at him. I have to force myself to shut up. My head reels with the possibility Dad could be dead before I can get there and adrenaline rushes through my body as I rock from one emotion to another.

"What is wrong with him?" I ask again.

"I told you, he has cancer of the pancreas. It's been pretty horrible. He's in a lot of pain and it's rough. He shouldn't still be alive." He sighs, "I know you wanted to be there."

I know he has waited till the last minute to call me. He's trying to have it both ways: I made him promise to let me know if that bastard was dying, and then he calls too late for me to get there. He needs to save his crazy sister from herself. I can't be mad at him for it.

He reminds me about being in the hospital for weeks. He brings up the two years I lost while I was on disability trying to pull myself back together. As if I have forgotten.

"I told them I would call you and let you know. But, there is no time. It's too late."

"Them?" I ask warily. "Who are you talking about?"

"Well, Bryan and his wife."

I'm not impressed. The endless machismo of my brothers is tiresome. Because I'm the only sister, it seems as though I can't make a decision on my own. I know without asking, it's all been discussed and the decisions were made concerning both my welfare and that of Dad's.

"None of you know me anymore. I haven't seen Bryan since he was ten! You are kidding me right? I am not going to discuss this anymore. I'm coming!"

The kids have begun coming through the door and they can tell by the tone of my voice that something is going on and instinctively they are quiet.

I say nothing and John finally gives me the necessary phone numbers. He tells me I can stay with Bryan if I insist on being down there for the funeral.

He repeats himself as if I didn't understand the first time, "I want you to know it's probably too late."

"John," I say evenly, "I don't care. I need to do this. I need to be there. You will never get it and I'm not going to try to make you understand now. And, for the record, I couldn't care less about any fucking funeral! I am not going there to say goodbye."

I breathe in slowly, trying not to scream at him for believing he can even begin to know what I need or don't need.

He sighs, "Okay, let me know what your itinerary is."

I can't wait to get off the phone and pack. Forty-three! I'm forty-three and I am still the bad one. I am still a child in an adult body. My turn has finally come. I have prayed for this day for as long as I can remember. The exhilaration is making it difficult to remain angry with John.

"I'll be there, tell them to count on it."

I hang up the phone and look at the kids. They are aware that my father is a very bad man. While talking with my brother I'd forgotten they were all there, probably hanging on every word. I look around forcing a calm that I don't feel and say, "My father is dying."

No one says anything and I sprint upstairs to pack. In my heart and soul I believe he must be buried with the things that represent his life. My journals, letters I wrote and received, The Letter and The List.

So, I will be seeing the baby brother I hardly know, Bryan. I do know he was in the Marines and that he may or may not have a baby. I haven't seen him since he was a kid. It occurs to me that I don't even know what he looks like.

John isn't going but he never said why. I'm baffled by that for a moment. I thought all my brothers remained in my father's circle. I thought they were all close, except for Gabe in the last couple of years. I thought they all did things like visiting, weddings, and other pseudo family stuff that I have ignored.

Gabe is not going to be there either. "Let that bastard rot!" he had said.

IN THE YEARS after I moved out, my parents divorced and Dad married Gabe's mother-in-law. So, along with a daughter in-law, he got himself a new little stepdaughter, Noelle, who lived with them full time. Gabe adored his little sister-in-law and in my eyes, she was nothing but a lamb brought to the slaughter.

I pull a couple of file boxes off the top shelf of my bedroom closet. As my arms stretch up, one of them falls on the floor. Thankfully, it's taped securely and other than a slightly crushed one corner, it is intact.

I pull down the picture of my little Annie Girl – the one I drew of myself as a little girl. It really is a horrible picture – a self portrait with forks stuck in me and blood everywhere. I can't leave without her. She always goes where I go. I put the boxes on the bed, wishing now that I hadn't used so much tape.

My husband always has a collection of knives on the dresser and I get one of the bigger ones, thankful I don't have to go downstairs for one. I am not ready to talk to the kids yet. I walk over to the top of the stairs and yell down for them to start their homework and to grab something to eat from the snack box.

I return to the bed, cut open both of the boxes and start looking through each of them, leaving some of the papers in the box and setting a few others aside.

My old therapist in the lower forty-eight kept copies of letters I had mailed. She thought I might want them later and gave them to me before I moved. I thought it was silly when I took them home but now for the first time, I realize I am grateful. They've been safely packed away for nearly ten years. I sift through the pile of papers, old doctor's bills, statements, disability papers and letters. I realize, suddenly, this box represents the disintegration and rebuilding of my life. It's all here like a road map: counseling, the hospital, losing my job, and the memories of a cruel previous boss.

During my breakdown in the hospital, I wrote The Letter and The List. Using those documents, I turned my father in for everything he did to me. First, I did it over the phone. While I was talking, I shook so hard I didn't think I would be able to talk. I managed to say the important things. I told them my therapist was with me. I told them I'd been abused; sexually, mentally, and physically. I said yes, I will write a letter as a follow up. Once the call was over, I sat motionless and terrified. I didn't talk to my counselor Ramona after. She was very matter of fact about it. I told her I was okay even though I wasn't. I believed I should be okay. I found the whole experience terrifying. I was sure he would find me and kill me. Nobody takes on my father. I had just taken the tiger by the tail and there was no turning back.

I was so tired after the call I went to my bed and cried myself to sleep. I guess it was a couple of hours later when one of the nurses came to wake me for dinner. I opened my eyes when she called my name and was instantly in tears and shaking.

"I turned my dad in today," I cried. "Oh my God! What have I done?"

The nurse sat with me till I was through it, holding my hand and listening the whole time.

"Now what?" I asked. "Can he get in here? Can he say, 'That's my daughter,' and get in?"

She assures me, "Honey, unless he is on the list you gave us, he can't get in. He would have to blow down three sets of locked doors to get to you!"

She hands me another tissue and pats my hand, "Let's get you ready to go eat. You'll feel better. You skipped lunch you know."

I wash up, brush my hair and follow her down the hallway. I'm nervous walking near the windows on my way to the cafeteria.

So, today, here in my hand is a copy of The Letter I wrote to the social worker as a follow up to my phone call after I left the hospital. I was so terrified she would not believe me, that I also wrote The List: pages upon pages highlighting all the things he had done to me.

Dear Sir,

Recently with the help of my therapist, I called in a case of child abuse from the mental health ward where I was hospitalized. I was told by your office that I needed to send a statement.

I also want to say that there is a minor female in the home where he lives, her mother is married to my father and she was made aware of my being molested and beaten regularly. I have enclosed copies of my journal made while in the hospital. It is a list of his actions which shows that this is a very sick man.

He raped me anally before I was ten and told me himself that I was six months old when "I" started it. Some of my memories are old and some are new. Please do something. He is a sick and brutal man. He is almost, if not a total pathological liar. I am thirty-three years old at this time.

I don't know what else to say. I hope the attached pages say it for me. I'm sorry this isn't more organized. It has been a difficult thing for me to do.

Thank you, Annie O'Sullivan

I LOOK AT The List now, all these years later, and think what a sad inventory to have had to take. What is saddest of all is that I believed they would call me a liar after they talked to my father.

I took The List to every therapist I worked with after. I would just hand it to them and wait for them to read it, thinking, 'Well, hey, this is me. Can you help? Can you handle it?'

I shake my head as I hold a copy of The Letter and remember how I felt writing it. I was afraid the person receiving it wouldn't believe me. I was in the hospital because my life fell apart and I didn't think this made me appear all that reliable. I certainly didn't feel safe at all when I wrote it. I felt as if I'd waged war with the gods and there was no turning back. This social worker was going to talk to my father and I was sure he would sweet talk her into seeing things his way. He has always been good at that.

I pick up an envelope with no name on it, and my hands begin to tremble as I realize what is in it. Just after I got home from the hospital, I wrote another letter to the person who had the power to help

Noelle - her father. Somehow, I knew Noelle would deny anything in it. If she had been anywhere near as intimidated by Dad as I had been, she would not risk it. For people like us, telling is always out of the question. The consequences are swift and severe if you have to go back home. You also learn that you can't trust strangers; because if you can't trust the people who brought you into the world, how can you trust anyone else? I sent that letter to her father anyway. I told him that I had reported everything that happened to me to a social worker and I gave her father all the contact information. I hoped for the best. I did it because it was the right thing for me to do, not because I thought it would make a difference.

I had hoped that someone would take a chance and do the right thing. I'd hoped Noelle could have a different life. I'd hoped that what I knew would happen to her, wouldn't happen. I'd hoped she would go and live with her father. I'd hoped for some sort of miracle. I had so many hopes...

I think it hurts more now to look at it. I look out the window at the mountains and wonder out loud if Noelle hates me. Does she hate me for not saving her from the beast I knew he was? Apparently, Child Welfare went to school and talked to her, I accomplished that much. Noelle denied anything was happening to her.

I feel the tears raining down my face as my hatred for my father comes full circle. I hate what he stands for. I hate what he did to me, to others, and all that he got away with. I had cried years ago because I couldn't help Noelle. I cried years later because as an adult she finally told what happened to her at the hands of my father. I cry now because of the futility of it all. I cry because he is finally dying and will finally get what he deserves, whatever it is. I can only hope it is something terrible.

I fold up the papers carefully and push them back into the bulging tattered envelope with the rest of the papers and get a nasty paper cut. The blood on the papers alarms me and for a moment I entertain getting a new envelope as I secure a rubber band around it. It snaps me out of the tears.

NO! This envelope is worn from use and there is a sort of comfort in that. I don't understand what I am feeling and decide it isn't important; but I will keep this tattered container of my most intimate and secret thoughts, memories, struggles, and pain. The blood? Hmph! This is the last time I will bleed over him. It's just a paper cut, but at this moment it symbolizes my life and war with the bloody memories on the inside, this last bloody fingerprint on the outside. I like it.

I finally find the suitcases way in the back of our large walk-in closet. They hadn't been used in years and I work up a sweat trying to get them out. They are dirty; and I swear loudly, "Damn things!" I get a couple of rags and some cleaner and wipe down a suitcase and a carry-on.

As I stuff the envelope and years of journals into my carry-on bag, I am so angry I'm shaking. I thought I was past all this anger? Will it always be here? Will it always hide there just below the surface? I can't bear to think it will.

My clenched jaw hurts. I will end up with another cracked tooth if I keep it up. I resolve to calm myself and take in a long slow breath.

I'm livid as my memories flood back...

SHORTLY AFTER I had come home from the hospital we had a little barbecue in my back yard. Gabe's wife looked down her nose at me and wondered aloud why anyone would talk about something like that happening to them. She assured me these things did not and would not go on in her family. It certainly did not happen to her sister or herself.

She went on admonishing me as if I were a child that needed instruction, "Nice people do not talk about this sort of thing and you made a mistake sending that letter to my father about Noelle. Nothing happened to her."

Then, in a moment of clarity I rarely experienced, I looked at her and said, "Your picture-perfect, flawless, successful, dream family married into my catastrophically fucked up one!" I turned and walked back into the house for a potato salad that didn't exist and cried.

I SMILE IN spite of myself now. I guess I am not nice. I never did stop talking about it and in the end, saw less and less of her. I never hear from her at all. Even now that she knows Dad did molest and abuse her sister, she doesn't talk to me. I tried to help and I am the bad one? She has never been angry at her mother who looked the other way. They are very close. As far as I know, she is only angry at me. I wonder if the guilt has eaten away at their souls.

I got a phone call from Gabe last year. I answered the phone and all he said to me was, "You can consider yourself absolved. Noelle told."

Of all people, I never would have thought that it would be Gabe who didn't believe me.

IN THE BEGINNING, Gabe was the only one that knew I had been admitted to the hospital and what I had done while I was there. I was humiliated at the idea; but I was falling apart. The minute my father found out, he started calling family members and friends. He couldn't wait to begin telling them I was crazy and in the loony bin. Apparently, this went on the whole time I was there. I was his crazy bitch daughter – the accuser.

He ranted at his mother, "She's bat shit crazy! She's telling people I raped her. Telling people I beat her! Telling people I sold her and gave her away for sex! You don't believe her, do you?"

When I got home, people came out of the woodwork. My mother, aunts, cousins, uncles, grandmothers and my best friend all called me. They didn't call to ask how I was doing. They called to persuade me to stop talking about my father and got angry with me when I told them I wasn't talking to anyone about it. Only Gabe.

I hadn't told anyone anything, but they all wanted to tell me what they thought about it. I was truly embarrassed.

My grandmother phoned and ranted at me in great frustration, "Why don't you just shut-up? No one wants to hear this ugliness about your poor father! He lost his legs, just let him alone! My son lost his legs! What is wrong with you?"

Indeed! What's wrong with me? My words were ignored. They never heard anything I said.

Not even my mother: she doesn't want to know. She didn't hear me then, and she doesn't hear me now. I realized that even as an adult, no one can hear me. I tried to defend myself against all their accusations unsuccessfully. I was still so broken when I came home from the hospital that I spoke with my therapist every day. I was in some sort of therapy every day, sometimes twice a day. I couldn't function. I had a daily schedule written out. Sometimes all I could handle was fifteen minutes at a time. I ran out of energy defending myself. I gave up. I changed my phone number and made sure it was unlisted.

It wasn't until I moved to Alaska, about a year after the hospital, that I found the courage to talk to my father. That wretched excuse for a human laughed at me. He found out I was looking for a lawyer – probably through one of my brothers since I wasn't talking to anyone else.

"The statute of limitations is up." He was nearly giggling, "You can't touch me! I already asked a lawyer!"

I didn't know that he had been to an attorney, but I had been to more than one with sad results. I didn't tell him that. The lawyers I contacted wanted several thousands of dollars up front. They said I would get nothing. No, he wouldn't even go to jail. They all told me it would be a civil matter. They were sure we couldn't make him pay for all the doctor bills. I wouldn't get any money. I wouldn't get anything but the satisfaction of someone saying he was guilty, if we won. I didn't want money. I wanted blood. I wanted him to go to jail. I was told that would not happen. At one point I cried, "What he did to me is a crime!" They would look at me, shake their head and apologize. I was stupid for thinking I could sue him, send him to jail, or even get a simple apology.

Well, that bastard is going to hear what I have to say now! I will be the last voice he hears before he expires and the devil comes to pick him up. I smile to myself. The last thing he hears will be me, telling him to go to Hell and rot forever, what a bastard he is, how much money therapy cost, how painful life can be, how broken I have been and how much destruction he caused.

I hear my husband coming in from work. I can hear him banging the snow off his boots. There is murmuring downstairs that I can't make out. I know the kids are telling him about the phone call.

I take a deep breath as I hear him trudging heavily up the stairs. His large frame is looming in the doorway. He hasn't even taken his coat off.

He is looking at the disarray in the bedroom with concern and a bit of alarm, "The kids say someone died."

"My father is dying and I am going to go down to his hospice."

My emotions are all over the map and brittle. I snap as he reminds

192

me that it's an expensive ticket, especially on such short notice, I know he doesn't want me to go, not for himself, but for my own well-being.

"I don't care how much it costs, and I don't care how we get the money." I say to him.

What little he knows about my family leaves him bewildered about why I want to go at all. He has never met any of them. I am exasperated even though I know he's trying to help me. There are no right words he can utter to me and he senses it.

I can tell he is thinking about his choice of words carefully and finally he asks, "Have you talked to Carol about all this? Does she think this is a good idea?"

It is absolutely the wrong thing for him to say to me and I'm instantly enraged. It's not fair to him but I don't care.

I shriek at him, "I don't want anyone telling me how to think or how to act or what to do! She is concerned! I don't care what you or anybody else thinks or feels about this! I'm tired of everyone wanting to manage me! I have to go! I have to! I will walk if I have to and that mother fucker better be alive when I get there."

He shakes out of his coat and comes towards me. He tries to hug me in spite of my temper, but I don't want to be touched.

I back away. "Please don't. I can't. I'm sorry."

Forget the gray and the numbness, I'm on the edge of a big black abyss and it's a terribly frightening place to be. I might fall in and never come back. I am barely holding myself together. I can't take any intrusion. I can't take any comfort, not even from my husband. In this, I am alone.

He realizes he is dangerously close to saying something that will cause a huge fight. It could be anything. He puts his jacket on the hook and helps me get ready. He says nothing.

He knows there is nothing he can say that will help or that I want or need to hear. I appreciate the silence. He goes downstairs to get me a reservation on the earliest flight out. I can hear him making the calls. I wonder for a minute what agency he is using. It doesn't matter. I am just grateful that he is handling it.

A few minutes later he is back in the doorway, "Tomorrow. You can leave first thing in the morning," he tells me with satisfaction. He knows that he has finally done something that pleases me.

Just that quick, and I will be on the plane. I am confident he will still be alive when I get there. It doesn't matter to me that John has said several times he should not still be alive. I zip my suitcase, and place it next to the bedroom door.

I am throwing some shampoo into the small bag in front of me. I ask my husband if he will get something from the top shelf of the closet. I can't reach it, and he gets it for me.

I open the suitcase back up and toss it in another piece of my past. My husband is staring at me looking a little confused and perplexed. It is annoying me, but I say nothing as I close the bag.

He finally sighs heavily and stares at me.

"What!" I ask sharply.

"Do you plan to take any clothes?"

I stare back at him for a minute. I look at the suitcase and I suddenly realize that I all I have packed is a pair of shoes, toothpaste and all my papers. I sit on the bed and I laugh out loud. I find it terribly funny and the tension is broken. He helps me pack some things for at least a week.

I won't leave till he is dead. I don't care how long it takes.

Going to Hell

I HAVE MADE IT THROUGH the ticket gate quickly and now I'm sitting in a deserted corner at the airport waiting for my flight, taking inventory of what I need to do both on this trip and in my life as well. I congratulate myself for having enough common sense to thank my husband for his patience and help. I also apologized for not being so difficult.

I called John early this morning to let him know when I would be arriving. He told me Bryan and his wife will meet me at the airport. Again, he reminds me I might not make it in time. For the first time in my life I want the bastard to live. I think my brother wants him to hurry up and die. It doesn't occur to me that John doesn't want me to tell Dad off. I can't imagine what this must be like for him, for Bryan or for Gabe. They still talk to him on occasion. There are things I want to say, need to say. I have to admit to myself that I am a little nervous about standing up to him.

My father is a genius at arguing. Even when you know he is going to lie, he debates, and you believe him. I haven't seen him for over ten years and I'm afraid I may not be resilient enough in the end. If I am not strong, he will crush me. I have to do this. It's the singular thought that I have been pushing away all night. I haven't shared my feelings with anyone for fear they would stop me from going. I have to do this. I don't even know why, but I will walk the three thousand miles if I have to. It's my turn to win the fight. I am not a very nice person because I am going to yell, scream and swear at a person who is dying.

I have talked to Carol. I assured her I am ready to do this. I wasn't really sure if I was when I spoke to her. But, I am now. Just because I am afraid, it doesn't mean I am not ready.

I have my envelope full of letters and my journals.

I brought a book to read. I brought some knitting with me in case I find myself having trouble sitting still. I've been here waiting for my flight for over an hour and I haven't read a word or knit a stitch.

I get up to wander over to the clock for the hundredth time when I hear them finally call my flight for boarding. I grab my things and head over to the boarding line.

The lady next to me says, "You look pleased. Are you going to visit family?"

"Why, yes, I sure am!" I smile at her. I show my boarding pass to the attendant and head into the plane. When I die, I am going to burn in Hell.

Settled into my seat, I begin rehearsing in my head all the things I am going to say. It's ugly. I am so full of hate, anger and poison right now. It's a boil bursting with forty-three years of confusion, lies, unhappiness, frustration, anger, grief and hope. Yes, hope. I'm hoping he is sorry. Is he?

In the innocent, deeply hidden part of my heart there is always this hope that one of my parents would be big enough, love me enough, to just apologize. That undying hope they would say, "I love you and I am so sorry I was a rotten parent." A hope for unconditional love. The bitter part of my heart knows to knock it off with all that silly mushy stuff, because it's not going to happen. The little girl that is still me can't accept that boat sailed for me a long time ago. I believe that miracles happen: people have epiphanies on their death beds. Maybe he will be sorry when he sees me.

My mind is racing all over the place as I stare out the plane window. I am going to tell him off. Then, when he sees how hurt I have been, how damaged my life has been, he will be sorry. Somehow, he will let me know he is sorry. Even then, will it be enough for me?

The flight attendant has brought coffee. I have taken my envelope out of the carry-on bag. The tattered, worn envelope that gave me that nasty paper cut not twenty-four hours ago. The envelope that holds The Letter and The List. Not even God can ignore a list like this. I want this envelope to be buried with him. I will set this list of all the rotten, filthy, vile things he did right on his chest. He will take this to God. This is the list to which he will answer to keep himself out of Hell. God might have ignored me, my prayers, and my messed up life; but God can't ignore a list so perfectly documenting the sins which attest to a man's failed life.

"You can't ignore this, God." I am murmuring to myself. I need to get hold of myself. Hopefully, the guy sitting in the seat behind me doesn't realize there is no one sitting next to me.

I might not have any faith in God, but I know there is one because there is a Devil, incarnate in the spawn that is my father. I'm angry at God today. I'm okay with that. I've been angry at Him for years and I have yet to be turned to a pillar of salt or struck by lightning. I smile at that thought, since God might have once tried to help me: years ago, Dad was struck by lightning. We lived in North Carolina at the time. It was a few months before he was in the explosion that took his legs off. There was a terrible storm, the sky turned dark and the rain beat down so hard on the roof of the mobile home we lived in, it sounded like pebbles. As my father ran from the car port to the house, it hit him! He stumbled, fell down for just a moment and got up and came running inside.

"Did you see that? Did you see that?" He bellowed. "Nothing can touch me!"

No, nothing could ever touch him. He just kept living. Lightning, explosions, drugs and car accidents, nothing could ever kill him.

"Well," I tell myself drily, "pancreatic cancer will kill him. What a horrible death; I sure wouldn't want to die of what he has."

All the years of therapy telling me I have to let it go. How? I don't know how to do that. It's outrageous to think I should forgive him! If a murderer comes in and wipes out the life of someone in your family or your friend, everyone goes to court. They get validation. They get to see someone punished. They get to pound on their chests. They get to point their finger and cry, "Guilty! Hang him!" Everyone feels bad for them and agree and cry out with them in outrage, "Guilty!"

My vicious, merciless, sadistic, rapist father, the child molester, wipes out my life and God only knows who else and I get told to let it go, forgive, move on, and get over it. "Why don't you stop talking about it?" people say. That statement annoys me the most because while I was in the hospital and after I got out and came home, I never said a word. He did all the talking and I was the one who got told to shut up! How did he do that?

If I wasn't being told to leave it alone, I was being told to have faith. Faith about what? How? Someone tell me how? I so envy those people who are so sure, so grounded in their faith that they can just hand their troubles over and God says, "No problem, I will handle this for you!" Should I have faith that God will make it better for me? Not so far. Should I have faith that all this was preordained? Should I have faith that I was chosen to live this hell? Should I have faith that everything happens for a reason? As a child, I cried myself to sleep asking God to help me. God abandoned me a long time ago. Now it's over, I am supposed to go find Him and feel better?

I didn't do anything wrong! I will never forgive my father or God! My family and God abandoned me when it mattered. I will never forgive.

I have a friend who tells me I should not talk about or to God this way. Well, I believe God understands and deserves my anger. I don't understand Him helping some jerk at church find their car keys when they pray for help. I don't understand most things people claim God helped them with. It's insulting to think that He would waste his time on trivial things like that. We have war, murder, rape, incest, hunger, lost children and lost souls and you stand up in church and say you were so special he helped you not be late by finding your keys! It's insulting to me, other survivors and to God. God knows me and He knows what I'm all about. I'm sure He's fine with that.

God must want me to put on my big girl pants and get up all by myself. So I will. I don't need Him to do my dirty work. I'm the big girl now and I'm on my way to usher my father to Hell.

The flight attendant is asking if I would like to watch the in-flight movie. I'm startled by the question, but glad for the distraction. "No thanks, I brought something to read." She smiles and goes on to the next seat.

I look out the window through the clouds to the land below mumbling with grim satisfaction, "It's my turn, you bastard."

I have my journals on the tray in front of me, coffee to the side and I begin to flip through the pages. I want everything fresh in my mind when I talk to him. Reading the journal is my rehearsal. I turn the worn pages to the first angry scrawled entry. I wrote it right as my life was falling apart, and as my therapist was coaxing me into the direction of a hospital stay. She assured me the journal was my secret. For the first time in my life, I trusted someone. So I wrote.

Four days later, just after my daughter's birthday, I was admitted to a hospital. I cried the whole day.

I close the journal and sit looking out the window again. I can feel the tears start and I take a couple of deep breaths trying to ward them off.

"I will not cry; I will not cry," I chant to myself. "Excuse me?" I look up, a little startled.

"Would you like something to drink? Coffee or a soft drink? You okay, honey?" The flight attendant looks concerned.

"Oh! Sure, coffee. Thanks, I'm fine." I force a smile.

She trots off to wherever she goes to get coffee and I look out the window waiting for her return pondering what I am walking into at the hospice. I think about my journal and the letters I have been reading and I am outraged all over again. The anger feels new and so does the pain. Will I ever get over it? I lower the tray that belongs to the seat next to me to hold my coffee as I see the flight attendant coming my way. Normally, I think airplane coffee is a vile brew not fit for human consumption. At this moment, it smells divine and tastes great. That sweet thing, she's brought me a cookie too.

I shuffle my papers, get comfortable in my seat and wonder if maybe I shouldn't be reading all this. It's a fleeting thought. I'm preparing for battle; of course I should.

As I turn the page over, I gasp. Oh my God! I forgot. My suicide note. There is so much pain in that letter. The disappointment in my family, my friends who stopped coming around, my old boss and his ignorant comments, another failed marriage, and my insecurities as a mother. I don't need to read this. It's nothing new. I started trying to kill myself when I was seven or eight. The reasons were always the same: I am not good enough; I don't know how to be good enough. My parents caused this pain. I am no longer the person who wrote this letter. I am no longer the little girl eating a bottle of baby aspirin. I finish my coffee and pick at my lunch.

I smile weakly to myself as I read the next entry:

OH MY GOD! I'm awake! I feel so sick! Oh my God, my head hurts! Alive! Now what? I need to call my therapist. And she will ask: Where is the evidence that this is true? I'm so tired of answering that fucking question.

I was furious! I remember making my way out to the kitchen and sitting at the table. I stared out into the back yard. I stared at my journal and the note I had left for the world. Now what indeed! I tried to kill myself and failed, again.

Yes, it's okay to smile about that all these years later. The note I left was so sad. I felt I had nothing left to give. My life had beaten me up and I was tired.

At the time I was so broken and so dependent on my counselors and people in my group counseling it didn't occur to me to just throw the letter away and pretend it didn't happen. I answered to people every day about my life as I lurched forward from completely shattered trying to put myself back together. I only felt more failure because I botched this too.

I can smile now because I'm past it. I can now find the humor in my failure. I can smile because, I'm here! That was the last time I attempted to kill myself. There were plenty of times it crossed my mind. There were plenty of times I seriously entertained the idea. My life was never that black again. Sometimes you have to laugh, or you will cry. I am tired of crying. As the plane speeds towards my destination, I vow, I am done crying.

I feel a headache coming on and lean my chair back and close my eyes. I think about the Critical Question: Where is the evidence that what you believe is true? I hated this question. I loved this question. When you can't trust yourself to recognize the truth of a situation you have to learn how. This was my acid test for my emotions and my perceptions.

My father told my brothers I am trying to ruin his life. He told my grandmother too. No one talks about what happened. They only talk about how it makes them uncomfortable. They don't ask how I am doing. They want me to shut up. At some point I realize that they don't even know me. I have ceased to exist for them. Cut out. Erased.

I have become the person to call every couple of months to complete the fantasy picture of a complete family. Then I disappear. I sit up and shift in my seat trying to get comfortable.

I shake my head and pull the seat upright. I search my bag for aspirin. I don't want to sleep deeply enough to have a nightmare on the plane. I have had little sleep and I could feel myself free-falling through memories and fragments of conversations, half asleep and half awake.

I feel like hurting myself. I hurt myself when the tension in my life became too much and I don't know what to do. Ten years later, I still do it occasionally. Sharp, quick pain releases something and allows me to go on and to feel like I'm going to be okay. I had moments that I reveled in euphoric joy at my success and then I would crash again into despair. It's all been so hard. As if I were a baby learning to walk, compelled, no matter how many times I fall, to keep going, lurching forward, falling and then getting up again.

I have not disappeared. I have not been erased. They will hear from me loud and clear before this is over. They were bad, not me. They were deaf. Well, I'm screaming! That's what babies and toddlers do. They lose their temper in frustration while they try to learn how to navigate the world around them, but no-one seems to understand them. CAN YOU HEAR ME NOW? I don't want to be this way! They stole my life and they think I am making them uncomfortable? How dare they? Ten years of struggling on so that I could sit on this airplane ready to confront him. Am I only brave enough now because he is dying? Does that make me a coward? If I am a coward, it doesn't matter. This is my last chance to make something inside me right.

I flip through a few more pages. I didn't remember writing about the affirmation exercises. I hated them but my kids loved them. They helped me post them all over the house. I remember there must have been over one hundred of them. I wrote them. The kids wrote them. I struggled to think of positive things, the kids didn't struggle, it came easy for them – bless their hearts. They were taped to mirrors, doors, walls, the refrigerator, windows, even the kitchen table and chairs and television remote!

The attendant has asked me to push the table up since we are preparing for landing. Suddenly, I can feel the adrenaline rushing through my body. I'm a little dizzy from the rush and it is nearly nauseating as it continues to wash through me and I consider that maybe I should have brought some Xanax or something. It makes me angry. Why should I feel like this? I had started to relax and now I'm angry again, and afraid.

"Kiss my fucking ass, God!" I whisper angrily as the plane begins to descend. "Don't worry, I'll do your job for you. I'll send him to Hell, I will. I will make a deal with the Devil himself if I have to."

As I stand to enter the aisle, the man who has been sitting behind me helps me with the bag stowed in the overhead compartment. I feel a little uncomfortable wondering what he has heard.

I smile, thank him and step out.

Day One

I T IS HARD TO SAY who arrived; me, the adult; or me, the child.

I've been stewing for twenty-four hours. I've had very little sleep. I'm tired and feeling wary. My sister-in-law is picking me up. I have never met her or even seen a picture of her. I stand looking around thinking this is silly. I'm the last one sitting at the baggage claim, I have her paged and walk over to a little coffee kiosk.

I find I am surprised a few minutes later when a small woman with a baby on her hip waves at me.

"I'm Stacey! You look so much like Bryan that it must be you! I heard the page you were here by the café!"

I laugh. I don't tell her I'm not sure what my brother looks like. He doesn't know me and I don't know what he has told her about me, so I am not going to volunteer much. She hugs me quickly and the baby, who looks remarkably like her mother, grabs my hair.

"A baby!" I exclaim. "I'm your Auntie!" I say to her; she is beautiful and I love her instantly.

"Do you want to go straight to the hospice or to the house first? I'm really sorry to meet you under these circumstances." She gives me a searching look.

I haven't thought about what to do. I stand there speechless over the simple question. She looks at me for a minute, "Let's get your bags, then we can get coffee and decide what to do." I'm grateful for the reprieve. At least someone has a plan because despite my stewing, I don't.

"Mmm, smells marvelous," I tell her explaining that it's my first time in a Starbucks. I go on, "They haven't descended on Alaska yet. We have Kaladi Brothers." I order a large double something.

Stacey laughs when I comment, "What I really need is a triple!" We plan to go to the house and drop the bags, then to the hospice. I feel a little like a fighter who has waited their whole life for this single match. I discover, I am ready.

It's like a beautiful summer day here in Oregon. I have the car window open and tell Stacey, "This is great! It's still winter in Alaska."

We arrive at the hospice quickly after a very short drive. We walk through the double doors, down a maze of hallways. I'm surprised that no one has stopped us as we walk through the facility. I begin to wonder if I can find my way back out, when she suddenly stops, "Here we are."

I stand there for a moment that felt like an eternity. This is it. I will go through that door and nothing will be the same. I will leave a winner or a loser. I will leave broken or whole. He could break me.

Crazy things are in my head. Should I say:

Hi Daddy!

Hi Dad! Devil been in yet?

Hi Dad! Met God? Talked your way out of Hell yet?

Hi Dad, I hear you called me a whore last week!

Hi Daddy! Are you sorry?

Hi Daddy! Do you love me?

Hi Daddy! Please love me!

Hi Daddy! Please see me!

Stacey's voice has broken into my whirlwind of thoughts. "He is in the bed there in the back side of the room."

I walk through the doorway into the room feeling like I'm six years old. It smells like antiseptic. It looks antiseptic.

I don't recognize my father. It's been ten years and he looks like someone else. My brain feels disorganized. His hair is thin and stark white. His arms are still enormous from getting around on crutches and in a wheelchair, but the rest of him is small. He is sleeping. I say nothing. Seemingly, our arrival has not disturbed him. He isn't hooked up to anything I can see except what I assume is a drug pump. He must love that, I think to myself ruefully. I find I can't stop staring.

The small man in the bed is not the giant monster of my memories.

He is very small, old, crippled and weak.

Stacey's voice from behind me jerks me from my thoughts. "He can't talk. Just a week ago we would bring the baby in and let her crawl on the bed. It made him so happy to talk to her; it's too bad she won't remember how much he loved her."

"Yes, it is," I force a smile. I feel brittle. He is dying, who cares what she thinks of him. Who cares what the baby thinks of him later? It doesn't matter to me right now. I am so focused on my anger, hate and disappointment. I am so focused that I am nearly numb.

Stacey chatters on about Dad's disease and illnesses over the years. I didn't know he had heart surgery or was diabetic. I didn't know but could have told anyone he didn't take his medication or follow a healthful diet. Did she just say he can't talk? I know he could talk a couple of days ago, since apparently he called me a whore!

My father lost his legs in a prank explosion that he caused and in the end it was the best thing that ever happened to him. She, along with everyone else who met him, believed he was a war hero and now she is telling me it was a privilege to know him.

My head is cramping and a headache is starting. She keeps talking, trying to make me feel better. She tells me my brother is devastated. It occurs to me she thinks I am grieving his imminent death.

I haven't had to listen to the pro-Dad propaganda for a very long time. It used to deeply hurt me, but now I find it tedious and annoying. Unless I want to start something, which I don't, I will have to keep my mouth shut, which I do. I get away with simple statements and gestures in the proper places.

The doctor has come into the room. It appears he knew I was coming and as he shakes my hand he inquires if I have questions. We step into the hall and he tells me that my father could pass at any minute.

"Frankly, I don't know why he is still alive. There are a couple of other doctors here that see him as well. I'm sure they will be happy to discuss any of this with you if you like," he smiles. "The priest has been in and he has already been given Last Rites. Now we're just trying to keep him comfortable with morphine until the time comes."

"Thank you for your time," I tell the doctor.

"You need anything at all, you let us know," he says as he closes the chart in his hand and walks away.

Stacey has to get the baby home and get ready for work and as she leaves, Bryan has come in. He looks tired. He is young, big and loud and seems to fill up the room.

He hugs me and asks, "How was your trip?"

"Okay," I sigh. "Travel is always tiresome. So, how's it been here?"

"Tough. He should have been dead a couple of weeks ago. We just keep waiting. He stopped talking the day John called you."

"Really?" Inside I am smiling, score one for me! Outside I am gravely listening to my brother. Bryan is the one who stayed with Dad after he got divorced from Noelle's mother and has taken care of him. I wouldn't have, nor would Gabe. John wouldn't have either.

"You want to go eat?"

"No. I think I will sit here for a while. I'm fine."

He tells me he will be back in couple of hours. Once he leaves, I pull a chair over to the corner of the room and sit.

After all these years I am alone with my father. He is small and pathetic in the hospital bed. All this white! White walls, white sheets, white blankets and his white face. He looks old and frail and he's only in his early sixties. He has awakened, however he doesn't notice me sitting in the room. His mouth moves slightly, a little like a fish out of water, but no noise comes out. His eyes are wide open in horror staring at something at the foot of his bed. Nothing else moves except his thumb, lightly and endlessly pumping on the drug machine. Anything to ease whatever discomfort he's in.

Seeing his reaction, I look over at the end of his bed. I don't see anything. There must be a bug on the end of the bed, I think to myself. I'm so sure something is there that I stand up to look. There's nothing, but my father is terrified! It's interesting, since I've never seen him afraid like this. I sit back down and watch him. I don't try to comfort him. I really don't feel much of anything but curiosity. There isn't anything there.

I have a couple of hours before my brother comes back. Dad hasn't noticed me in the room. Between the morphine and the cataracts I heard he has, I figure he is nearly blind. I had taken out my knitting but I left it lying on the table by the chair. I just sit here beholding what is left of my father.

Two hours have passed. Bryan comes into the room smiling big and the first thing he does is grab the drug pump and hit it a few times. He comes around to the other side of the bed.

"Hi, Pop! How are you doing? I'm here. I love ya! How ya feeling? I told you I'd be back! I won't leave you alone!"

I can see he loves Dad as much as I have hated him. I can't imagine that. What's it like to love your father and be sad that he is passing away? I'll never know.

Bryan turns to me, "How are you doing? You okay? You talk to Pop?"

"No, I don't think he knows I'm here."

Bryan turns back to Dad and asks loudly enough for anyone down the hall to hear, "POP! Annie is here! Yeah! She came to see you!"

"He knows you're here," he announces confidently.

I laugh and tell him, "Now the whole wing knows I'm here!"

He chuckles, "He's a little deaf."

"I'm sure he is thrilled to know that I'm here," I respond dryly.

"Really? He seems to be a little confused," Bryan laughs. "You ready to go get some sleep? It must have been a long day for you traveling and all." As kind as Bryan is, he just doesn't understand what I'm going through. In the past, he has made it abundantly clear that he doesn't believe my claim of incest, violent repeated rapes and beatings. He has simply decided it isn't true and there will be no conversation about it. I resent this. I let it go. I seem to be letting a lot go today.

We stop to get something to eat before going back to Bryan and Stacey's home. The conversation comes around to what arrangements need to be made. There will be no funeral. There is no one to come. Dad has a girlfriend who will come if we pay for it. How sad to live a life so selfishly that in the end, there is no one who gives a damn. No friends, no family. There is no one who cares enough to stand up and say something about his life. I can't imagine this! Not even his old military buddies or sick neighbors come to see him in the end.

I talk with my brother about the baby and get ready for bed. Going up the stairs, I wonder if I will be able to sleep. I forgot my pillow and I hate strange beds.

I'm asleep before I even have time to toss and turn.

Day Two

IT'S JUST BEGINNING TO GET light outside as Stacey leaves for work, the baby is going to a sitter, and Bryan is also running off to work but will drop me off at the hospice. I told them last night that I will spend the day there. I'd be fine. I don't mention I have things to say. I am feeling excited and terrified all at the same time. I pound down a couple of cups of strong coffee as I get ready to leave. My brother and I don't talk on the way, but as he drops me off at the curb he offers to come back at lunch time if he can. I assure him I will be fine.

I enter the hospice and after a few minutes of wandering around lost I get some directions. I take a deep breath and enter the room to resume my seat in the corner. I've been sitting a couple of hours doing nothing but staring at him when a nurse comes in.

"Bath time!" She sings out. She is babbling about what a privilege it is to take care of a war hero like my father.

"You must be so proud of him!" she exclaims. "It's good when someone has led a good life."

"Who told you that?" I ask trying to keep the shock out of my voice. "Who told you he was a war hero?"

"Why he did, honey!" She went on, "He was quite a talker up to a couple of days ago! Told me all about all those boys he has, too."

"Did he? How nice for him." I reply drily.

I marvel at how easy it is for me to slip into my old self, agreeing with whatever lies came out of people's mouths just to keep peace.

Christ help me! What if she asks who I am? I quickly decide she probably won't. This is simply idle chatter while she does her job.

What I really want to know is if he told her he has a daughter. I want to know if he said he was sorry. I want to know if he is afraid of going to Hell. I want to know if he ever loved me, if he really ever loved anyone. I certainly can't ask her! The words are dying inside of me. It will be embarrassing. It hurts. I thought I was past that. Goddamn it!

My father can't even talk and I am, again, nothing but a helpless little girl. I begin to self-talk. I begin affirmations. I begin looking at the clock and figuring out my life in five minute increments to make it all manageable. I am a good person. I didn't do anything wrong. I was a child. I was not in control. I am in control now. I am strong. I am smart. I am… The affirmations are in my head and I find I can listen and think at the same time.

Why do I care? Why?

The nurse is talking to Dad now. Telling him he has company this morning.

"There is a fine looking young woman here to see you! You look dashing! Don't look so worried!" She laughs and smiles at him as she pulls the curtain open from around his bed.

Her comment that he is worried is not lost on me. What does he think? Is he afraid of me? She brushes his hair and his teeth for him, blathering the whole time that she is getting him ready for his guest. She never mentions it is his only daughter. Clearly she doesn't know he has one.

At this point I don't have the heart to tell her that I am the last person he wants to see. She finishes her job with a bright, "Goodbye, see you tomorrow!"

Another woman comes in. I can't believe how busy this place is. She introduces herself as the social worker. Bryan told her I would be here. She goes into her speech about a life lived well. I should be proud of him. I can't listen.

"I can't listen to this anymore." I stand up. "I'm sorry but this is the biggest bullshit fabrication I have ever heard. I'm sorry. I know that this is your job, but I can't listen to this."

My father looks like he is asleep again. Maybe he is dead. I look closer and see his chest still moves.

She looks quite stunned.

"Look. It's not your fault. It probably doesn't really matter to anyone but me, but I don't want to hear anymore. The man over in that bed was the meanest, nastiest, most self-absorbed and selfish, evil man I ever knew!"

I stand and point at him as I go on evenly. "He was no hero. He got all his medals because he bought them. He made up stories. If anyone would bother to check it out they would discover he was not in the Special Forces all those years he talked about. He did not serve in all the places he claimed. He lost rank as often as he made it. He was a cook. He was a troublemaker. He was a coward and more. It's an insult to anyone who ever served, including me, that he is called a hero!"

"Maybe we should go down to my office," she says quietly.

We walk silently down the hall. I am trying to compose myself and I am sure she is doing the same. She looked quite astonished at my outburst. I'm not sure I blame her. We settle into her small little office.

"Would you like some water, coffee, anything?" She asks as she gets out her note pad.

I smile politely, "No thanks. I'm not even sure why I am here. I shouldn't have said all that to you. I should have just let it go."

I'm wondering why she is planning to take notes. I decide to ignore it. He will be dead. I've got years of therapy and people sitting in front of me with note pads.

She regards me with curiosity and softly remarks, "You appear to be angry."

I pause for a moment. I recognize the tone. This is not my therapist. This is not Carol who I trust and always answer as best I can. This woman will never be my therapist. She will not confront my father.

Yet, I smile and feel guilty as I answer, "Yes, I guess I am. It's sad isn't it? Everyone thinks I am here to pay my respects and say goodbye to my father. I'm not. I believed I came here to see him to Hell. But, right this minute I am not sure why I'm here at all."

I tell her everything and she can't scribble fast enough.

Three hours later, I come out of her office exhausted and looking for coffee. Now they know. Maybe they will stop treating him like he is special.

I shake my head as I mumble to myself, "She took notes? I can't believe she did that. I wonder what she thinks she will do with them."

I decide it doesn't matter. I don't know if she believed me or not, but I'm sure she will quit fawning over him when I am around. I smile at the thought. Surprisingly, it's enough for me.

I return to the room. He is again looking at the end of his bed a little to the left and again I find myself compelled to look. I see nothing. He looks terrified. As I sit down in the corner I realize he has focused on me. I know he now sees me and he looks even more frightened. It is quite clear he can see me. He's made eye contact. He is scared of me! Who would have ever thought? Suddenly I feel tall as I stand up to observe him better. It's an odd feeling.

I pick up my envelope from under the chair and move closer to him with The List.

I suddenly remember he is nearly deaf in one ear and I can't remember which side.

I stand to say that he has to listen to me. It's my childhood, my life, my pain and my truth. At the moment I feel as worn out and full of holes as the envelope. I stand to tell him I have things to say and he has no choice but to listen.

I stop halfway between my chair in the corner of the room and his bed. As I stare at him, I abruptly realize there is nothing left to say to him. It's like I've been hit with a bucket of cold water. It's just paper. It's just my paper. He was there. I was there. What am I going to tell him he doesn't know? What am I going to tell him that he would even give a damn about? What am I going to tell him to make him see me, hear me or feel the pain he has caused? What can I say that will make me real to my father?

After so many years of dreaming and rehearsing this moment, on the very edge of saying it all; without warning, I realize that in the end I have nothing to say. It's a stalemate. Nobody wins.

I slowly walk back over to the chair and do nothing but sit there. I say nothing to him. I wonder why I came. Maybe my brother John was right after all and I shouldn't be here. I'm exhausted. I cry soft tears. I am so alone.

When I sit back down Dad lost interest in me and is again focused on something near his bed. It appears he is looking at something closer. He isn't looking at the end to the left any longer, but on the left side of the bed. It was as if it was closer to him. If I could see it, I would swear it came around the bottom corner. It's an odd sensation. I want to get up and look. I don't though. I can see quite clearly from my vantage point there is nothing there. The room is quite sparse.

I hear the door whoosh open. The doctor has come in to check on him.

"How are things going?" He asks.

"Hmm, interesting question," I reply. "He keeps acting like there is something he is afraid of at the bottom of his bed. It's been going on since I got here."

"Yes, we have noticed his agitation. There doesn't seem to be anything we can do for that. At first we thought there was something on the bed. Changed the sheets and blankets, but it did not help."

"Does this happen often? I just took a class and we were reading about near death experiences. Have you ever witnessed anything like this?"

"Well, sometimes they go hard and sometimes they don't. Some see things like loved ones, and others see something ugly. Some just pass as if there is nothing at all. Your dad seems to be going harder than most. Depends on your beliefs, I guess. One theory is that they hallucinate; another is that they are met by someone or something to usher them to the other side. I don't know what really happens. Of course, none of us will know for sure."

He concludes his examination and I ask, "Well, how's he doing? Can he hear me?"

"Oh yes," the doctor assures me, "his brain is still there. It's a terrible way to go. If he is awake, then I am sure he is aware. I don't know what is keeping him alive. He should have been gone a couple of weeks ago. His insides have gone to stone with the cancer. We can't even feed him. His kidneys have failed. He stopped passing anything a couple of days ago. There is nothing left. That IV hydrates him and allows morphine for pain."

It does sound like a dreadful way to go. I have nothing to add to the conversation nor do I know what to ask. I stand there simply looking at the doctor. He seems to understand and places a hand on my shoulder, "I'll be in again tomorrow." He smiles and steps out.

I can't help but think about all the times I prayed for God to let him die a hideous, long and painful death, alone. I got the first part, but I guess he isn't going to die alone since I'm here. That might be worse for him than being alone.

Bryan catches the doctor in the hall and I can hear them talking for a moment. As my brother comes through the door he asks if I want to go eat.

"No, I really haven't thought about it."

"All you've had is coffee since you got here!" he exclaims.

"I'm okay, not really hungry." I sigh. "I know I should eat though. Where are Stacey and the baby? Want to go get something?"

Bryan tells me he has to go pick up the baby and Stacey will be at work. We decide to pick up a pizza and go back to the house. He says he will run back over to the hospice with me when she gets home.

We are both drinking strong coffee and not saying too much. I pick at the pizza, but really have no appetite. It's an uneventful evening.

We return to the hospice, Dad is sleeping while we are there. Bryan doesn't want him to die alone. He promised Dad that he wouldn't let him die alone and has gone to great lengths to keep his promise. If he isn't at work, he is here. I have to admit, it's admirable to keep his word to the old bastard. I wouldn't. Then again, I haven't promised anything.

Bryan is clearly going to feel the loss and will miss Dad. John and Gabe apparently don't care. I believe my mother is tap dancing back at her house across the country.

Me? I've discovered I don't know how I feel.

Day Three

ISTOPPED FOR A TRIPLE shot espresso on the way in this morning. I find my way to the room without a hitch and I don't bother to pick up my knitting. I leave it in the bag on the floor. I have a book in my lap, but I don't even pretend to be reading it. It's just something to hold onto. I've been here a couple of hours already just watching him as he sleeps or wakes.

I wonder what it's like to be like a regular person whose parent is at death's door. I wonder what it would be like to sit next to the bed and lay my head on it. What would it be like to hold my father's hand? He can't talk. He can't move. Maybe I can just pretend he loves me and wants me to do that. It's an irrational thought brought on by exhaustion. Between all the coffee, and lack of sleep and food, I don't realize that.

Before I understand what I'm doing, I quietly drag the chair over to the bed. I sit on the edge of my chair, watching him sleep right up close. His eyes are the same. The rest of him is foreign. I don't know how long I have been sitting here studying his face. I'm so tired. I lay my forehead on the edge of the bed for a minute. The sheets are cool and feel good as my head is throbbing with a headache. I must have dozed off. Startled, I lift my head and look around.

Holy shit! He is staring at me and he is clearly afraid!

I chuckle and stand up. "Don't worry Dad, I'm not going to put the pillow over your head. You worried I'm going to suffocate you?" I find this quite funny. I stretch and walk around to clear the cobwebs and drag the chair with me back to my corner. Like fighters in the ring, he has his corner and I have mine.

I turn back around and look at him. He is again preoccupied with the end of his bed. I'm still standing there studying my father when a priest comes in. "Still here is he?"

"Yes." I don't really know what else there is to say. I smile, "What if I said no?"

He chuckles and puts out his hand. "I'm Father McCarthy. I'm guessing this is your father." It's more of a statement than a question. Who else would he find standing here in the middle of the day?

"Yes, yes he is."

"I hear you are having a bit of difficulty and thought I would come down and see if there is anything I can do for you." The priest is elderly, round, wrinkled with white hair and crinkly, kind eyes that look like they have laughed a lot. He is remarkably patient as he waits for me to say something.

"Do for me? I'm okay. Why do you think I need anything? The social worker must have spoken to you," I tell him. "I'm not really a Catholic." I say this as if it sums up everything. I smile trying to make light of the situation, "I'm not sure he is either."

Father McCarthy nods patiently. "That's okay, if everyone was really a Catholic they wouldn't have much use for me," he chuckled. "And yes, the social worker spoke to me for some time. You made quite the impression on her. It must hurt that he didn't tell us he had a daughter."

I take this in and dismiss it. I don't want to talk about that. "Are you the one who gave him Last Rites?" I ask, "Did you give him Confession?"

"Oh yes…"

I cut him off. "Did he confess everything?" I'm holding my breath. This suddenly matters a great deal to me.

"Well, I can't say if he did or didn't. He had the opportunity and that's all I can offer."

"Then he didn't. If he had you would have been shocked! You would have to assume that he told you everything even if he hadn't."

Tears begin to flow down my face. I'm not really crying. There's no sobbing. No gasping for air. Just buckets of tears.

He crooks his head and says to me softly, "What is it?"

"He is going to go to Hell. My father is going to go to Hell!" Now

I am crying in earnest and the priest is patiently standing with me, letting me cry.

I gain control of myself and he asks me why I think that. It's not something he usually hears.

I tell him, "He is a vain, selfish, self-serving man. He is a murderer, a rapist, sadist, and a pedophile. Only God knows how many people he has hurt in his life." I walk over to my envelope and as I pick it up I begin to cry in earnest again. "In here is The List of things he did to me! He did awful things that have damaged me. There is physical damage that will never go away! I came here to see him to Hell." I sob and gasp for air. "I-I-I w-wanted h-him to burn in H-H-Hell! And I have waited forty years for it to happen!"

Father McCarthy leans forward and in a whisper he ask me, "And now?"

I cry out, "He is going to go to Hell! He deserves to go to Hell! I don't want my father to go to Hell! I don't want my blood going to Hell! I'm all confused! Why couldn't he be a little decent? How would you like to know your father went to Hell? What if it were your sister or brother? This is not how it is supposed to be!" I cry. "He is supposed to go to Hell and I am supposed to be avenged by it! I'm supposed to feel better! I am supposed to be pleased!"

I am bewildered at my sudden flood of feelings so contrary to everything I have held on to all these years.

I tell the Father after I have calmed down, "I do not want my father to go to Hell."

I turn and point at the bed. "Look at him. He sees the Devil's minions coming for him down there at the foot of his bed and still he makes no move for redemption of any kind."

We talk about Dad's behavior here in the hospice. We are just sitting there when suddenly Father McCarthy sits a little straighter and says to me, "Think of one good thing about your father. Tell me just one good thing."

I don't know where he is going with this but the tears start again as I desperately race through my memories and can think of nothing. I cannot think of one redeeming action.

I look at Father McCarthy feeling little desperate.

"Just one thing..." he repeats softly.

I feel myself crumple as I sob, "There is nothing, I just can't think of anything."

He lets me cry for a while patting my shoulder, with assurances that I can't hear or comprehend. I finally stop and begin to regain control of myself. He continues to magically hand me tissues from somewhere.

"Well, it is what it is, huh?" I try to make light of the situation and my behavior. I am more than a little embarrassed at all this emotion over Heaven and Hell. I spent most of my life at odds with God. If something bad happens and He doesn't stop it, it's because of free will or maybe because he works in mysterious ways. If something good happens He gets all the credit. What a racket. I wipe my eyes and nose with yet another tissue.

Father McCarthy smiles at me like he is an angel himself. "You don't know?" he asks.

I am still wiping my eyes and trying to make sure I don't have mascara all over my face. It's a silly thing to do. It was cried away over an hour ago. I feel embarrassed at the outburst of tears and I still don't have very good control of myself but he has my complete attention with that question.

"Don't know what?" I am wondering to myself, did something happen over the ten years that I don't know about? Did he donate money? Help someone? This is all unlikely.

The priest placed his hand on my shoulder says to me, "Look at me."

I look up and I gaze at his face. I see his crinkled eyes and bushy eyebrows and as I watch him, he said the words that would bring a tear to my eye for the rest of my life.

"My dear child, there was good in him. The good in your father... was you."

Day Four

I'M DESPERATELY TIRED. I SLEEP a few hours, then get up and go to the hospice again. Thank goodness for espresso! I am convinced it must have been invented for just these types of occasions. I wave goodbye to my brother from the door of the hospice with my triple shot in the other hand.

I walk through the double doors wondering how much longer this can go on. I am beginning to think maybe I should just go home. He might linger for weeks. My family needs me. I have other things I should be doing. I will call home this evening and we can talk about it. I've had enough.

But, I have found out that my Uncle Clay is coming in on a flight tonight. I am looking forward to seeing him, and I think he's coming for my sake, and not necessarily that of his brother. Right now, this is looking like another long day of waiting. For what, I don't even know anymore. I thought I was waiting for him to die. I thought I was going to tell him off. Now I don't know what I am waiting for.

I attended all those years of therapy, counseling, groups and discussions about forgiving. I bet they told me a hundred times that I needed to forgive him. Well, I won't. I didn't do anything wrong. Carol tells me forgiving is not forgetting. She says it will be very difficult for me to move forward if I don't forgive him. I don't get it. He should be the one saying he is sorry. He is the one who should be begging for my forgiveness. There must be something wrong with me. I can't do it. He is nearly dead and I still can't do it!

So, coffee and my untouched knitting in hand, I walk through the maze of hallways to his room. I go to my corner of the room and sit.

I watch and wait.

Stacey comes in later in the day with the baby for a while. She tries to talk to Dad, let him see the baby. She thinks he sees her and is happy to do this for him. We sit and visit for a while. She has taken the rest of the day off. Bryan comes in and we all sit around. Bryan talks to Dad as usual in his booming voice convinced that he hears and sees all he says to him. Maybe he does. What do I know? I'm certainly not talking to him. I don't know if he knows what is going on or not.

Bryan tells him in his jovial voice that he is picking Uncle Clay up from the airport at dinner time and they will come straight to the hospital. He reaches over to the medication pump and hits the button several times. He laughs when he sees the look on my face. "It's okay, he likes it!"

"I'm sure he does," I reply dryly.

Bryan entertains us with a few stories. I laugh in spite of myself. This baby brother I don't know and who hasn't spoken to me in years is funny and likable. He has stuck to his beliefs that the accusations of sexual abuse were lies. He was not beaten, he was not molested; or so he claims. He sides with my father. He made it clear a while back that I was a liar. So I am cautious in my growing like for him.

Bryan was so young when I left home, that I have no idea how he was raised. I don't understand what would have happened to cause his life to be so different from the rest of us. I can only guess at what his life was like when my mother sent him back to my father after they divorced. She is aware of what generally happened to me, although I haven't told her any detail and she never asks.

Bryan leaves to pick up our uncle at the airport. We always look forward to seeing this gentle loving soul who is so different from my father. As Bryan leaves, he makes a lot of noise about it, and one would think it was about to be a party instead of a death watch.

Stacey and the baby stay with me and Dad.

We are talking about babies and my kids at home when suddenly the bed shifts, startling us both. We look over and the man in the bed who can't move or talk, is suddenly flailing his arms about wildly! I fear that the IV is going to come out or he is going fall out of the bed with all the thrashing. My thoughts are not making any sense.

"WHAT THE HELL!" We both shriek and stand up. Stacey has

the baby on her hip and I have dropped the book that was in my lap to the floor.

It feels like the whole room is in motion. Stacey starts for the door to get a nurse and I move towards the bed, I put my hand up to her and I unexpectedly cry out, "Stop!" It stuns me as it comes out of my mouth.

Stacey looks at me as if I have lost my mind but she stops anyway. I don't know why I said it and I don't ponder it at all. I keep moving over to the bed.

As suddenly as it started, it stops. He is quiet and motionless again. It almost feels as if he never moved and it was all just our imagination. I lean over my father and peer right into his eyes not more than six inches from his face. I realize those are the same familiar eyes I looked into my whole life. Those cold, unkind eyes are unmistakably focused on me, attentive, clear and without emotion. I look into them, brown and green like mine, but flecked with a yellow that I don't have. Our eyes are locked. He suddenly looks like the father I remember, not this white emaciated creature I've been sitting with these long days. Suddenly, I am not afraid and I feel tall.

"Can you see me? Do you know who I am?" I ask. It's important. I want to know that I am real to him.

His eyes close and his head nods. The movement is slight but he nods yes.

"Daddy? Can you hear me?" I ask only inches from his face. I ask again a little louder, the question I have longed to ask, "Can you hear me now?"

I hold my breath waiting for an answer to everything I want to know. Can you feel my pain? Are you sorry? Do you love me? All the venomous poison that a lifetime of hate, anger, pain and resentment has fermented and grown in my heart, that has screamed inside me for all these years without voice, is suddenly only a whisper in this void where only he and I exist. I don't ask about any of those things. I know the answer in this moment. I only ask, "Daddy? Can you hear me? Again, his eyes blink slowly and his head nods almost imperceptibly, yes.

There is no bed, hospital room, machines, or other people. I am encapsulated in a void that is only my father and I. Everything has fallen away.

I cannot stop staring, I cannot break the contact. I can't hear anything else. I am inches from his face for an eternity. We are connected.

Startling myself, I hear myself speak again. "It's okay, I want peace too."

He struggled to nod his head, then closed his eyes and died, and as he did, a primal scream came from me.

I felt the sensation of the air leaving the room. The curtains never moved. The temperature didn't move up or down. The air is still but I felt it, a swooshing out of the room and down the hall. Something awful came for him. It was inevitable.

I cry. I cry for what should have been. I cry for what will never be. I cry for what I will never get. I cry for my father's soul which I am sure went to Hell. I do not cry because I will miss him. It has only been a few moments but it feels like a lifetime has passed and I realize the room is in motion.

I cry because it feels as if the powers of the universe kept him alive to see who I am. I cry because I believe God finally answered my prayer. I'm aware of something powerful and know it will take some time for me to sort it out. Stacey has called for help. He is gone. My brother and my uncle come in right behind a nurse who comes into the room and tells us what we already know.

"Oh my God," says my uncle softly. "My brother is gone." He doesn't cry.

My brother is thunderstruck. "I was supposed to be here! I missed it by a minute? I PROMISED!" He lumbers out of the room without another word.

I am trying to tell him what happened, but he isn't listening. I suddenly realize my brother has lost his father and I can't fathom the feeling of loss that he has. I only lost the fantasy, the hope of having one. That door just got slammed in my face. I didn't really lose anything but the hope. In a strange way, I envy my brother.

Uncle Clay waits a few minutes and then goes out and finds Bryan. I leave my brother to grieve and go down the hall to call John and Gabe and let them know it's over. I think that's what I'm supposed to be doing. What am I supposed to be doing? Why the hell am I always worried about what I should be doing? That word needs to be eliminated from all languages on this planet.

I sit in a chair by the phones for a few moments to collect myself. I'm crying. I grieve for what never was and what now has no hope of ever occurring. I take inventory.

There will never be an apology.

I will never have a father.

It's over! The waiting is over. Waiting for someone to do the right thing by me is over and there is freedom in that.

Whatever happens to Dad now is out of my hands. It isn't up to me. It's up to me to live a good life, make good choices, take care of my family and be a good person.

But, the apology was part of my inventory, and I wanted it very badly.

I wander down to the bathroom and splash some water on my face, then come back to the pay phone. I sigh as I pick up the phone and insert quarters.

John takes the news well. He wants to know if I am okay. I assure him that I'm fine. "Did you call Mudder?" he asks, using his pet name for her.

"No, should I?" I find myself surprised at the thought.

"Maybe you should… I guess she'd want to know he is gone, they were married for twenty-five years!"

"Hmm, well, okay. I'll take care of it."

"Hey! Are you sure you're okay? You sound like you've been crying?" He asks.

"I'm good, yeah, I've been crying for days. Not for him, for myself."

"Yourself?" He doesn't understand and I don't feel any need to enlighten him.

"John, trust me, I'm okay. I will call you later when I know what is going on. I don't know where it goes from here. I guess I should help Bryan with some sort of arrangement. I'm going to call Gabe, unless you want to."

He doesn't.

Gabe is angry. "Don't call me and mention that sick bastard's name again!"

"I just thought you'd —"

He cuts me off. "I hope he is rotting in Hell. I don't care if he is dead! Why are *you* even there?"

He hangs up before I can answer. I sit staring at the phone thinking about how awful this is.

Why am I doing this? Why am I thinking of making some sort of arrangement for him? It doesn't make any sense, and I could just get on the next plane and go home. I fall back on a tried and true rule from my youth. What would my family do? They would get on the next plane and never look back. So... I will stay and help Bryan get through and somehow bury the beast that is my father.

I decide John is probably right, and I call my mother assuming she would like to at least know.

She also says, "I hope he rots in Hell for a long time. When is the funeral?"

"I don't think there will be a funeral."

She harrumphs and hangs up.

I get off the phone and ponder my situation. Here I am, of all people, seeing to my father's final details. Here I am, of all people, forgiving. Here I am, of all people, moving on.

Here I am, and I know that God hears me and is smiling somewhere.

Life Today

MY WHOLE LIFE I HEARD, "You can never go home." Every time I heard it, I would think, "Why would anyone want to do that?"

I made a couple of trips home over the years to see my family because I felt this is what "normal" people do. For the most part, it was miserable.

While my father was alive, I had to worry about my kids and never ever took my eyes off of them. I had to listen to the yelling and screaming that went on until my hands would shake. I felt the need to pretend I was happy to be there. It took years for me to realize I was pretending, as I always had, to have a happy, loving family.

I tried mightily to believe I was loved and had value. I thought if I pretended hard enough, somehow I might find the family for which I hoped so fervently.

My parents divorced when I was in my late twenties. The house was heavily mortgaged, and burned to the ground shortly after and just before it was to close to a new buyer. The whole thing was suspicious to many and the gossip flowed, as it does in any small town. I was told the house went up like flash paper and happened to be well insured. Some of the locals marveled at how much money my father got in the settlement. I found this interesting as insurance is not something my father would have willingly paid for. Dad was gleeful. He couldn't stop talking about how much money he made off it.

I made a trip shortly after all this and while in the area drove out to the old property. It was a beautiful piece of property the day we arrived. I saw that Dad had subdivided the land. I saw some shacks and old trailers dotted around. It looked like a slum. The burnt foundation of the house we had lived in remained. Ugly memories seemed to have permeated the very ground on that ten acres and from that sprung more trash and ugliness.

About twenty years later, I was traveling to a class reunion and decided to detour and go check out the old property. I was going to stare down the old ghost one last time.

I'd forgotten how pretty the area really is. It hadn't really changed, yet it was different. Some very expensive homes had been built, sprinkled in amongst the timeworn ones that I remembered. Picturesque wineries now dot the old road all the way to the end. This, in comparison to my memories of home brewed potato vodka!

The grade school now has a fence all around it and a new playground, but looks mostly the same. From the road I could still see the corridor that led to my seventh grade classroom, the multi-purpose room where I graduated from eighth grade and attended my first dance.

The corner store is still there. I went inside and was surprised to find a quaint little deli with a room in the back for concerts. There were posters upon the walls commemorating past performances and those coming. We used to live at the end of this paved road. Go to the T in the road, turn right, and follow it up to where it splits three ways....

I saw my old tree stump and stopped to take a picture of it.

Things changed. Instead of three roads there was only one. I pass familiar and unfamiliar on the short stretch of road and come to a gate. A very large, very sturdy, eight foot gate, clearly and ominously posted:

NO TRESPASSING.
TURN BACK.
VIOLATORS WILL BE SHOT.

I had no trouble reading the sign. I recognized this as the edge of the property where we too once had a gate; although, not nearly as impressive.

It's raining. My windows are fogged up and it's hard to see. I get out of the car and walk up to the gate. In front of me are apple orchards with bright green leaves and very red apples still on the trees. It looks like a picture in a book. Even in the rain, it's so beautiful. I look to the right and see nothing but apples trees. I wonder for a moment if they would really shoot me. I feel I have every right to be here. I am glad to have on hiking boots as I boldly climb the chain link fence. Hanging on to the NO TRESPASSING sign I get a really good look around over the trees.

It's beautiful. The art of Mary Engelbreit comes to mind. The trailers and shack houses are gone. The entire property is covered in apple trees. The foundation to the house that burned is gone. I look to the left and expect to see the old house that was used for the horrors of my adolescence. Further up a little rise would be the old mobile home. The shop of horrors is gone and so is the old mobile home. In their place is a beautiful farmhouse and more apple trees. Even the hay field that was next to us now had apple trees. Apple trees as far as I can see. It was as if all the pain and ugliness that had happened here was used as fertilizer to make something nourishing and beautiful.

The land has been repaired. I have been repaired. I climbed down off the gate, sat in the rain and sobbed.

I WAS ONCE just a little girl and fragile. I was my parents' incomplete thought in the backseat of a car at conception and the creature that would go on to ruin their lives. I was without substance, courage, appreciation or understanding. I believed I was treated so badly because I was so very wicked. I was self-serving and cared only for my own survival. I would not risk extra whippings or death to save my younger brothers. I believed I was an undeserving and worthless character whom my parents did not want and of whom God disapproved. As I got older, I was just as certain I would live, grow and leave my hell. If I could endure to escape that household, I would do something that mattered. I would make my life matter somehow. For our lives to matter, even if it is only in some small way; isn't that what we all want?

A FEW YEARS ago I told my mother I was trying to write a book, and her flippant reply was, "I am quite sure it will do very well. It will probably be a bestseller. I want you to know I will never read it." She went on to say, "Change a few names and dates. No one will know." She never even asked what it would be about.

My mother has been remarried for nearly thirty years. She doesn't write or call. I used to write, but she doesn't write back. I still call once a month. It's painful. I try to talk to her about my kids and grandkids but she still isn't interested. The last time I saw her was over fifteen years ago. She told me then that she would never see me again. I drove away from her house that night wondering if she was right. I guess she was.

I worked hard to have a relationship with my mother in spite of everything. It was a conscious choice made with the awareness she would never give me what I needed and I would have to accept what little she had to offer me. My mother doesn't know her grandchildren and has never seen her great grandchildren. Recently, she told me she was pronounced The Best Grandma in the World, by someone that I am not related to and have never met.

I don't talk to my brothers. Any loyalty we could have had broke away long ago. They don't understand me. They don't know me. I have nieces and nephews that I don't know. I have been estranged from cousins, aunts and uncles since I was a child.

Bryan told me indignantly, "You have ruined the family name by writing this book."

MY RELATIONSHIP WITH God is still complicated. I believe that both of us are okay with that.

For most of my life I have argued with God. I have sworn at him. I shook my fist when I felt I was abandoned. I was told to pray and God would help me. He did not. I continued to hear from people who believe God has especially blessed them and answered their prayers. I wondered for years why he didn't answer mine.

I don't believe God allowed for this to happen nor do I believe He saved me. I don't believe He allowed me to come through the fire. I can already hear the cries of outrage that I can say such things.

God did not make me good. I choose to be good. God did not allow my father and his friends to do what they did to me and others. They elected to be depraved.

I believe there is punishment for life lived in depravity without regard to others. Free will is the test every human will pass or fail every day. My parents failed. However, the punishment is not mine to dish out. Even if I had managed to get all this into a court of law, I would have little if anything to do with their punishment. It's not up to me to decide what will happen to anyone. I once thought it was. Once I let that go, I discovered my freedom.

AFTER TWENTY-FIVE YEARS of stops and starts, and half a dozen schools, I graduated from college with a double masters and 3.85 grade point average. It was transforming. I felt free, worthy and special for the first time in my life. I was fifty-three years old.

My children are happy and successful. They have wonderful relationships in spite of me dragging them through my crazy life. They don't always understand me, and I tell them I thank God for that.

My life today is a testimony to what a therapist said to me a long time ago, "Take care of yourself, love your children and be sure they know it, and things will work out. You are breaking the cycle in your family."

TODAY, I LIVE alone. Marriage has not worked well for me. I've been married more times than I care to admit. I tell my friends jokingly that my picker is broken. I would like to have a relationship, someone to grow old with, travel, share things and laugh with, however, that doesn't appear to be my path in life.

I don't choose men very well. As an adult I've been beat up, cheated on and verbally abused. I have dated an alcoholic who had more issues than I have ever had. I was married to a man who said to me, "All I can see when I look at you is what happened to you."

When I first started this book, I was back in therapy for about a year. Since then, I went back to school, worked, moved and have been writing. I don't put much effort into romantic relationships right now. I'm fine with that.

I PAINT, KNIT, try to go to the gym, make dolls and visit my kids. I have great days and bad days at work like anyone else. I have many friends. I have a rewarding job that I believe matters. I have put my life out there for all to see.

I do radio shows and blogs. I write to people on the internet. I constantly try to communicate to those I have never met and hold my hand out to them when they need someone to say… "You are normal, your experience was not."

I talk to other survivors who are just embarking on their journey. They are scared. They are looking at themselves in the mirror for the first time and don't know who is looking back. Sometimes, I cry for them and the pain they must go through to heal. Sometimes, I laugh out loud at their triumphs.

By telling my story I have spoken out for those who can't and to clear the way for others to tell their story.

I have sobbed over discoveries in recent years as childhood friends have shared their stories with me. My father affected so many lives. One of my friends wrote an essay which is included in this book. She never told until now. It set me back a little. My true friends have all shared their memories to validate me and themselves. There were no harsh words and no accusations. What greater gift can one receive than understanding and acceptance?

I HAVE MEDICAL issues. I have the neck of a seventy-eight year old arthritic woman. It aches. I get headaches. I take medication to fend off the pain and the inevitable deterioration. I am evaluated annually with x-rays and MRIs and adjusted with physical therapy.

I have had internal physical issues that accompany being raped at a young age.

I occasionally still fight off depression, but I've learned to recognize it and take care of myself. I have learned I deserve to take care of myself. I deserve to be loved, respected, cherished and will no longer accept less. I have not taken medication for depression in over five years. It was once thought I would never be able to stop taking them.

The tragedy is not in what happened to me. The tragedy is in the numbers of stories like mine.

By the time I was offered a contract to publish I could wallpaper my entire home with rejection letters. My family, though excited at the success of my story, worried about the safety of their children and families. So we chose a pen name, Annie O'Sullivan, my great, great grandmother. She came over on a ship from County Cork, Ireland when she was eighteen years old. When she left the ship, she became Annie Sullivan; she thought it sounded more American. Although, I only know her from the stories I was told, I greatly admire her courage. She was spunky, brave, and full of life and fire.

I no longer hide my story. In that, there is freedom.

I always said if I got my book to paperback I would use my real name. That turned out to be a challenge. Now people know Annie O'Sullivan. Annie O'Sullivan is that little girl you have been reading about. I am no longer her. I am forever indebted to her for assuming the worst parts of my existence, allowing me to grow out of and survive the madness.

Change will probably be something I strive for until my last breath. I want to be better, for myself, for my family, and for those still reading. I want the world to be a better place, in however small a way, because I did something right. I want it to matter that I was here.

Annie O'Sullivan
1955-2004

Debora Boudreau
1955-Present

I have not had a night terror or nightmare since the death of my father.

I have as my legacy beautiful daughters, a handsome son, beautiful, healthy, and happy grandchildren.

Life has gone on,

and;

against all odds, life is very good.

ABOUT THE AUTHOR

Annie O'Sullivan served in the United States Marine Corps and following a hospital stay and two years of disability she went on to log ten years of counselling. She has since earned two Masters degrees and maintains a rewarding career in land management. Her own successful family has grown to include multiple grandchildren, dogs, cats and several fish - all happy and well.

Against The Odds: Life Is Good.

ACKNOWLEDGMENTS

I would like to offer my sincere appreciation to my many friends who believed in me, cried with me and never stopped believing that surviving my experience has significance and purpose. There are so many people to thank over the seventeen years that I tried to make this story readable, that I can't list them all here. I want all of you to know that your endless patience in reading and re-reading my work looking for lapses is appreciated. This made all of you, not just me, a voice for those who, in their isolation, shame and pain, have none. I would like to offer a special thanks to Teresa Dixon for her editing and elimination of those pesky commas that just kept growing and those late nights we fell asleep looking for them, and her husband for not complaining. I love you both more than you know. You have become my family.

Michelle Halket, my publisher, I offer my sincerest gratitude for taking a chance on this book. On my story. Lives have been changed, and you were the conduit for that. Nothing is more important than leaving the world a little better than we discovered it. Thank you also for giving meaning to what happened to me, for making it matter that it happened at all. Finally to Ellen L. Ekstrom, fellow author and soul, who put on the finishing touches. Thank you for all your efforts and hard work to make this book happen.

My deepest gratitude goes out to Carol Lambert, Deborah Geeseman, Teri Merz and Ramona Farmer for literally saving my life and teaching me how to find myself when I was lost. Each of you forced me to look in the mirror and see who I was and who I could be. You are all, wherever you may be today, responsible for the stillness and peace in my soul. Thank you does not convey what my heart holds for each of you, but it's all I have.

RESOURCES

Childhelp USA
National Child Abuse Hotline (Multi Lingual)
1-800-4-A-CHILD (1-800-422-4453) TTY 1-800-222-4453
www.childhelp.org

Department of Children and Family Services
1-800-25ABUSE (1-800-252-2873)

National Youth Crisis Hotline
1-800-HIT-HOME (1-800-448-4663)

National Runaway Switchboard
1-800-RUN-AWAY
www.1800runaway.org/parents/resources/

National Domestic Violence Hotline
1-800-799-SAFE (7233) TTY 1-800-787-3224
www.thehotline.org

Rape Abuse Incest National Network
1.800.656.HOPE
www.rainn.org

Boys Town Suicide and Crisis Line
800-448-3000 or 800-448-1833 (TDD)
Short-term crisis intervention and counseling and referrals to local community resources. Parent-child conflicts, marital and family issues, suicide, pregnancy, runaway youth, physical and sexual abuse, and other issues.
www.boystown.org

Covenant House Hotline
800-999-9999
Crisis line for youth, teens, and families. Gives callers locally based referrals throughout the US. Help for youth and parents regarding drugs, abuse, homelessness, runaway children, and message relays.
www.covenanthouse.org

** Resources were verified at time of publication but may change without notice.

State Hotlines

Alabama	800-650-6522	TTY 800-787-3224
Alaska	800 478-4444	907-586-3650
Arizona	800 541-5781	TTY 602-279-7270
Arkansas	800 482-5964	800-269-4668
California	916 445-2771	800-572-2782
Colorado	303 727-3000	800-799-7233
Connecticut	800 842-2599	
Delaware	800 292-9582	800-799-7233
Dist of Columbia	202 576-6762	202 727-0995
Florida	800 962-2873	TTY 800-621-4202
Georgia	404 657-3408	800-799-7233
Hawai'i	808 832-5300	
Idaho	800-669-3176	
Illinois	800 252-2873	877-863-6338
Indiana	800 562-2407	800-332-7385
Iowa	800 362-2178	800-942-0333
Kansas	800 922-5330	
Kentucky	800 799-7233	
Louisiana	504 925-4571	888-411-1333
Maine	800 452-1999	866-834-HELP
Maryland	410-857-7322	800 799-7233
Massachusetts	800 792-5200	877-785-2020
Michigan	800 942-4357	800 799-7233
Minnesota	612-646-0994	800 799-7233
Mississippi	800 222-8000	800 799-7233
Missouri	800 392-3738	800-799-7233
Montana	800 332-6100	800 799-7233
Nebraska	800 471-5128	800-876-6238
Nevada	800 992-5757	800-500-1556
New York	800 342-3720	800 799-7233
New Mexico	800 432-2075	800 799-7233
New Jersey	800 792-8610	800-572-7233
New Hampshire	800 894-5533	866-644-3574
North Dakota	800 799-7233	800-472-2911
North Carolina	800 662-7030	800 799-7233
Ohio	614 466-0995	800-934-9840
Oklahoma	800 522-3511	800 799-7233
Oregon	503 945-5651	800 799-7233
Pennsylvania	800 932-0313	800-692-7445
Puerto Rico	800 981-8333	
Rhode Island	800 742-4453	800-494-8100
South Carolina	803 734-5670	800 799-7233
South Dakota	605 773-3227	800-572-9196
Tennessee	615 313-4746	800 799-7233
Texas	800 252-5400	800 799-7233
Utah	800 678-9399	800 799-7233
Vermont	802 241-2131	802-223-1302
Virginia	800 552-7096	800-838-8238
Washington	800 562-5624	800-562-6125
West Virginia	800 352-6513	800-799-7233
Wisconsin	608 266-3036	800 799-7233
Wyoming	307 777-7922	800 799-7233

National Society for the Prevention of Cruelty to Children
A list of organisations concerned with the protection and welfare of children in different countries, arranged A-Z by country.
www.nspcc.org.uk/Inform/research/directories/worldwide_wda54664.html

Australia Child Abuse / Child Protection Hotline
1800 700 250

Canada Child Abuse Hotline
1-800-4-A-CHILD (1-800-422-4453)
www.stopchildabuse.ca

India Childline
Tel: 1098
childlineindia.org.in

United Kingdom - National Society for the Prevention of Cruelty to Children
Tel: 0808 800 5000
www.nspcc.org.uk/

German Society for Prevention of Child Abuse and Neglect
Tel: +49211-4976800
www.dgfpi.de/

Centre Français de Protection de l'Enfance (CFPE)
(French Centre for Child welfare)
www.cfpe.asso.fr

OTHER RESOURCES

National Association of Anorexia Nervosa & Associated Disorders
630-577-1330
www.anad.org/

National Mental Health Association
1-800-273-TALK
www.nmha.org/

National Center on Elder Abuse
1-800-677-1116
www.ncea.aoa.gov

Parent Hotline
1 800 840 6537
www.parenthotline.net/

Poison Control
1-800-222-1222
www.aapcc.org

Thursday's Child's National Youth Advocacy Hotline
1 (800) USA KIDS
www.thursdayschld.org

National Center for Missing and Exploited Children
800-843-5678
www.missingkids.com

Child Find of America
800-I-AM-LOST (426.5678)
www.childfindofamerica.org/

Substance Abuse and Mental Health Services Administration
findtreatment.samhsa.gov/TreatmentLocator/faces/quickSearch.jspx

The American Counseling Association recommends five ways to help with coping AFTER a crisis situation.
1. Recognize your own feelings about the situation and talk to others about your fears. Know that these feelings are a normal response to an abnormal situation.
2. Be willing to listen to family and friends who have been affected and encourage them to seek counseling if necessary.
3. Be patient with people; fuses are short when dealing with crises and others may be feeling as much stress as you.
4. Recognize normal crises reactions, such as sleep disturbances and nightmares, withdrawal, reverting to childhood behaviors and trouble focusing on work or school.
5. Take time with your children, spouse, life partner, friends and co-workers to do something you enjoy.

Printed in the United States
by Baker & Taylor Publisher Services